AF333897

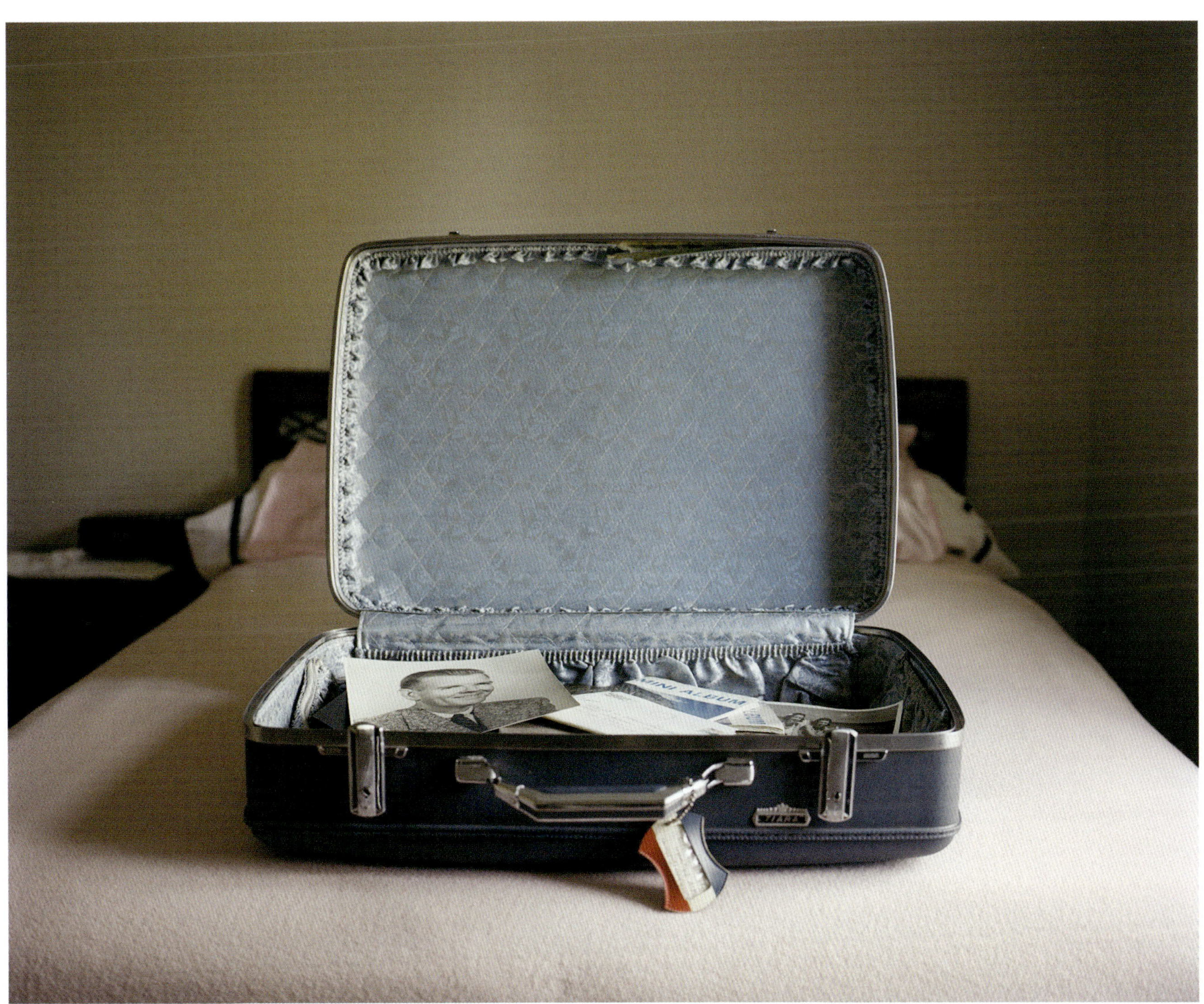

WHAT DID THE DEEP SEA SAY

SARA MACEL

KEHRER

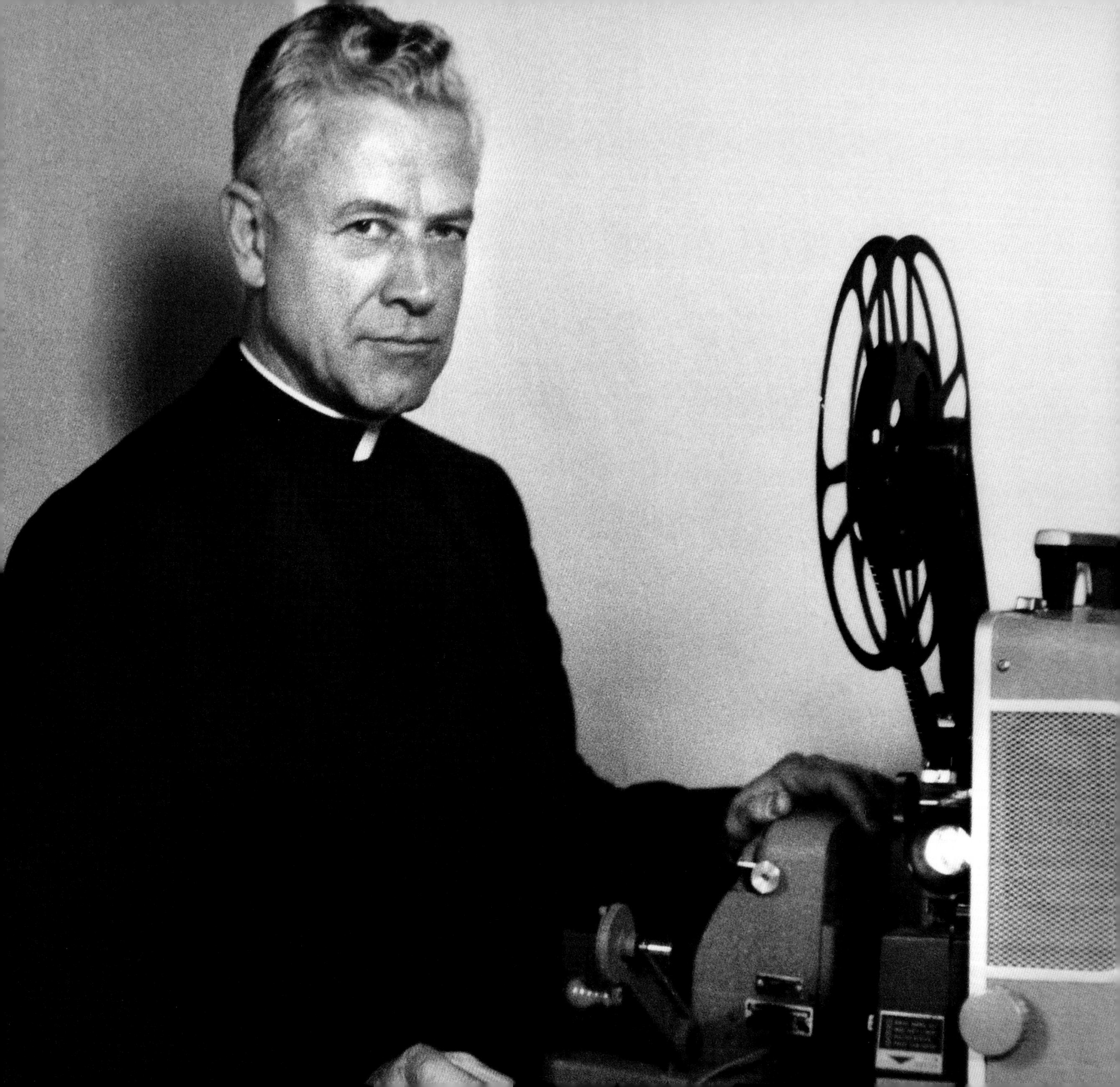

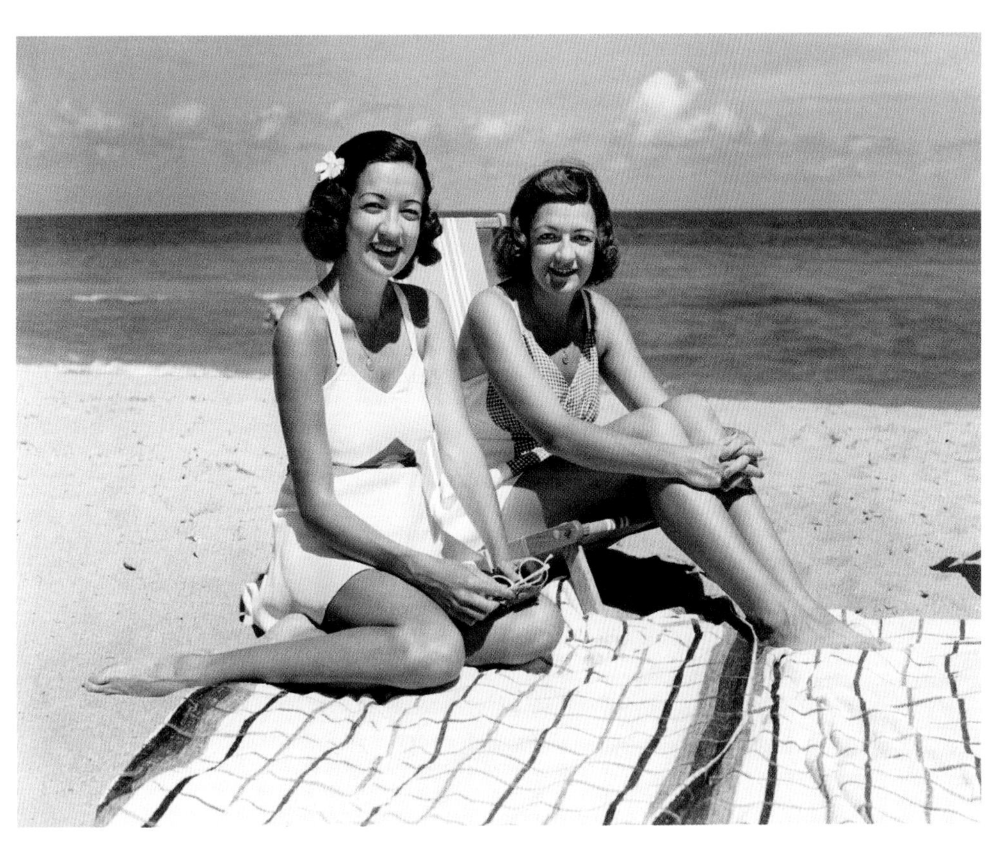

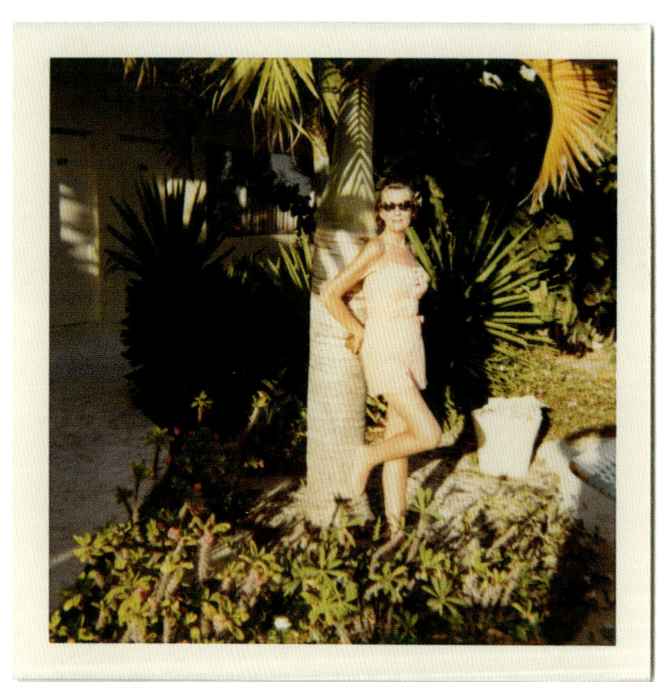

For years, I have had the same dream: My family and I are all swimming in the ocean. They laugh in the waves and float on their backs, blissfully unaware of the deep dark shadows that circle us below. I am the only one who sees the sharks. But instead of alerting them to the danger, I dive down to get a closer look. And that's when I wake up.

In 2014, I discovered a suitcase full of photographs and negatives that belonged to my deceased grandmother Carolyn. The same handsome shirtless man appears in many of her photos. I only knew him when he was much older but instantly recognized him as our family priest. Upon closer investigation, and after questioning my mother about the suitcase's contents, I came to find out that before she became a wife and mother of six, Carolyn had a whole life in Hollywood, Florida that she never talked about.

The place was called "Dream City" when founded a hundred years ago, but it never quite lived up to its name. Curious to know more, I spent the next four years researching Hollywood and traveling there to revisit scenes from Carolyn's life.

My grandmother and I weren't close. The strained relationship between her and my mother meant that we were kept apart for most of my life. She died twenty-six years ago when I was too young to know the questions I now wish I could ask. Everyone who knows what happened on that beach in 1944 is gone.

I'll never know the whole story. This is just part of it. The rest is for her to keep.

Her and the sea.

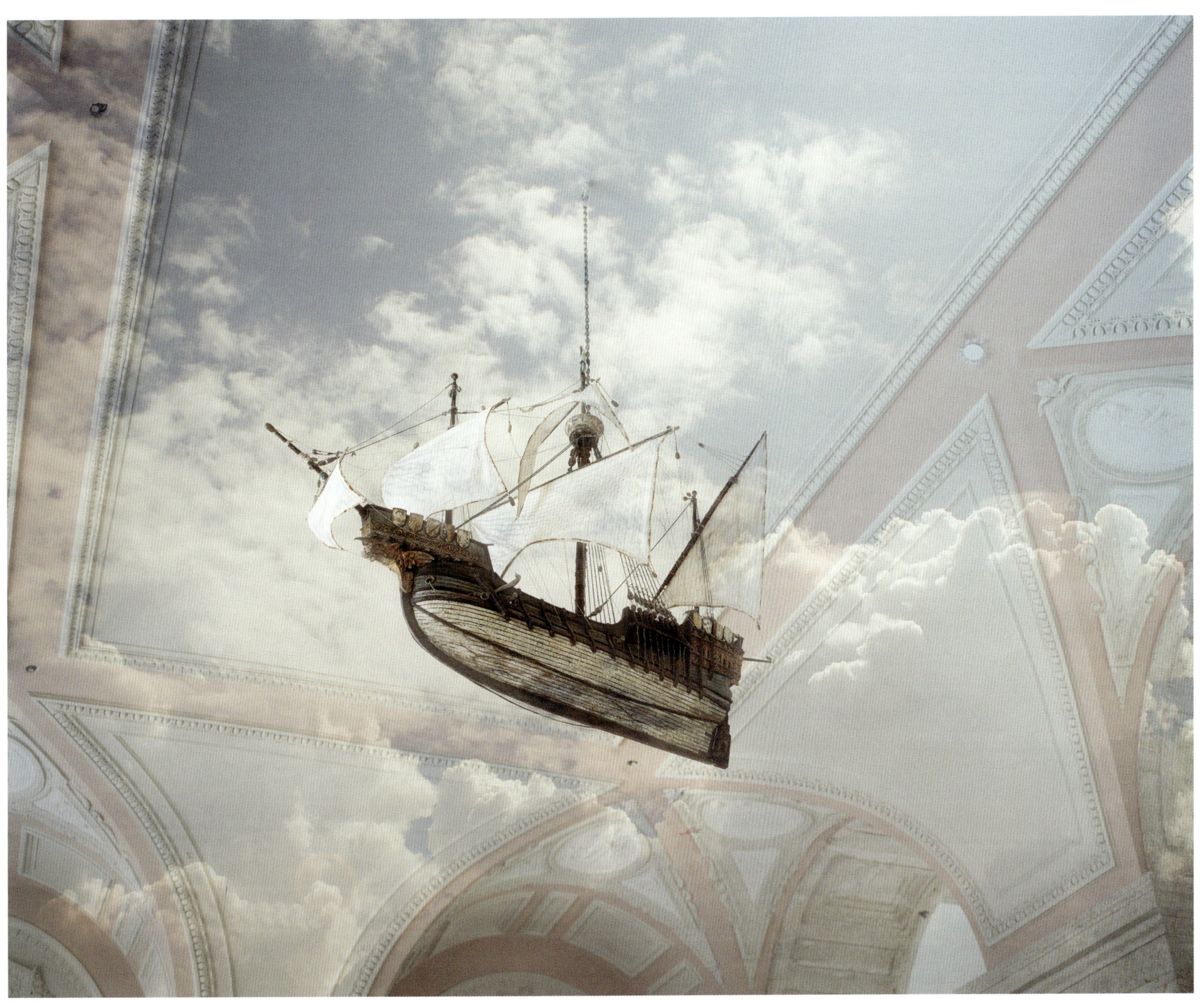

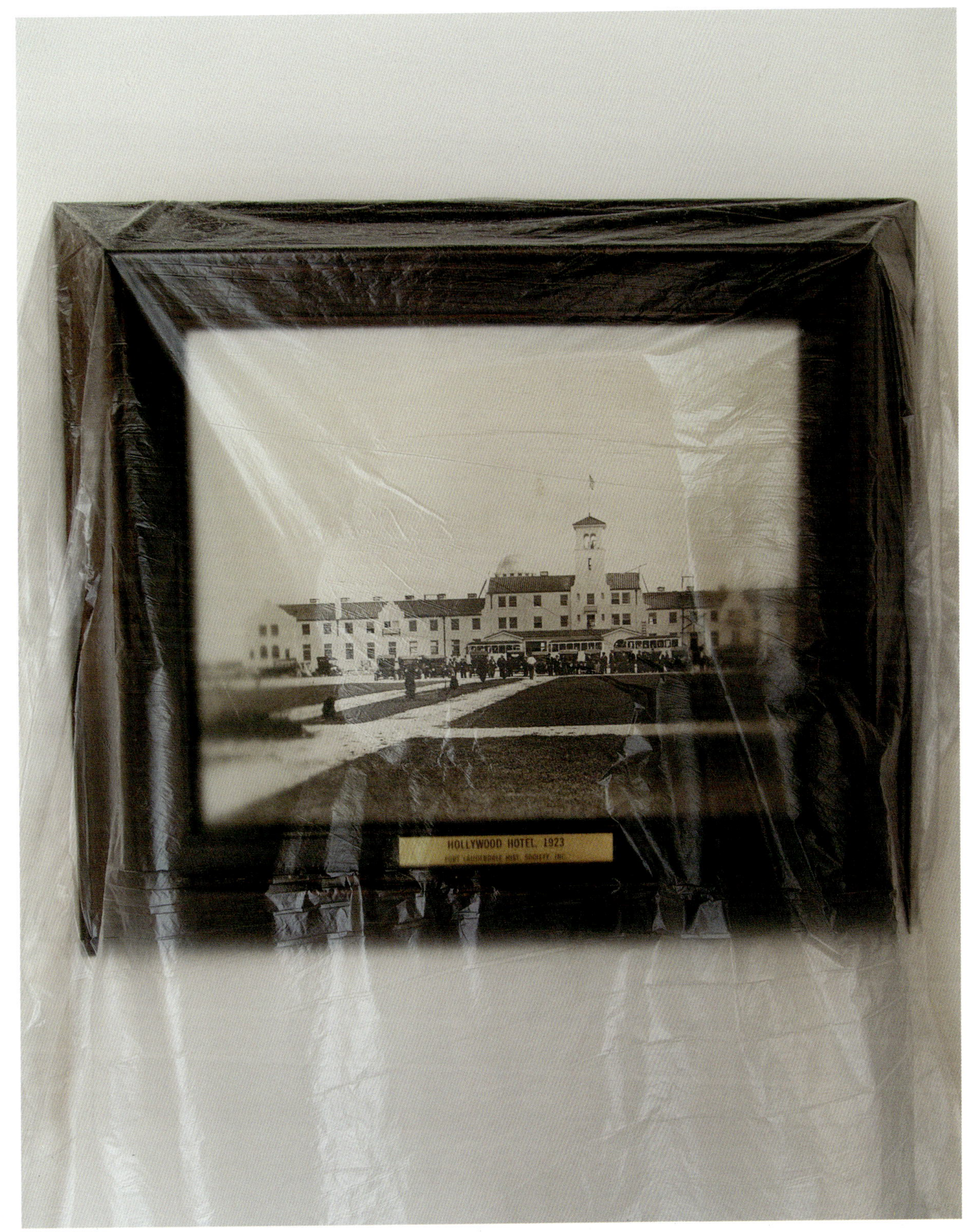
HOLLYWOOD HOTEL, 1923
FORT LAUDERDALE HIST. SOCIETY, INC.

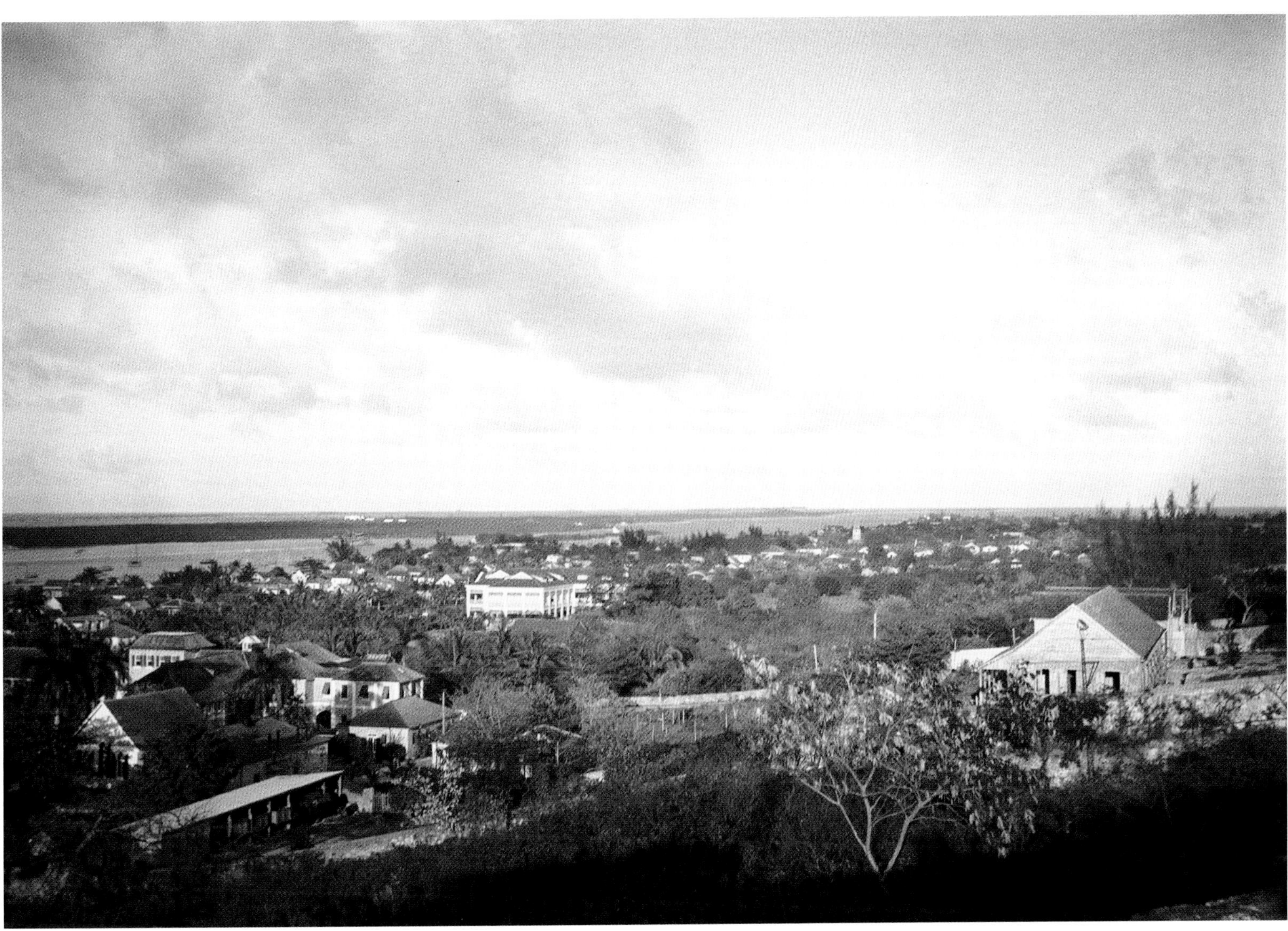

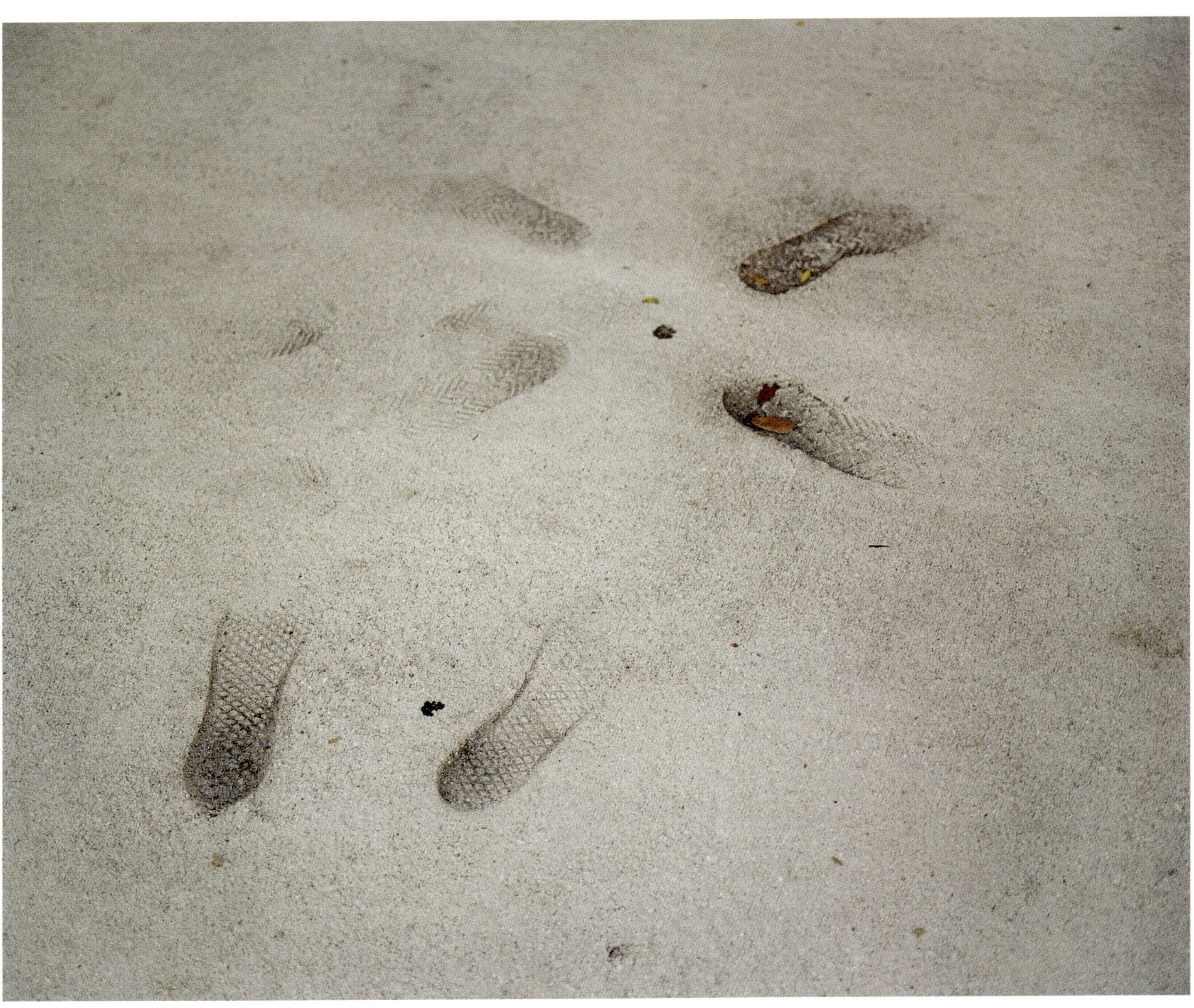

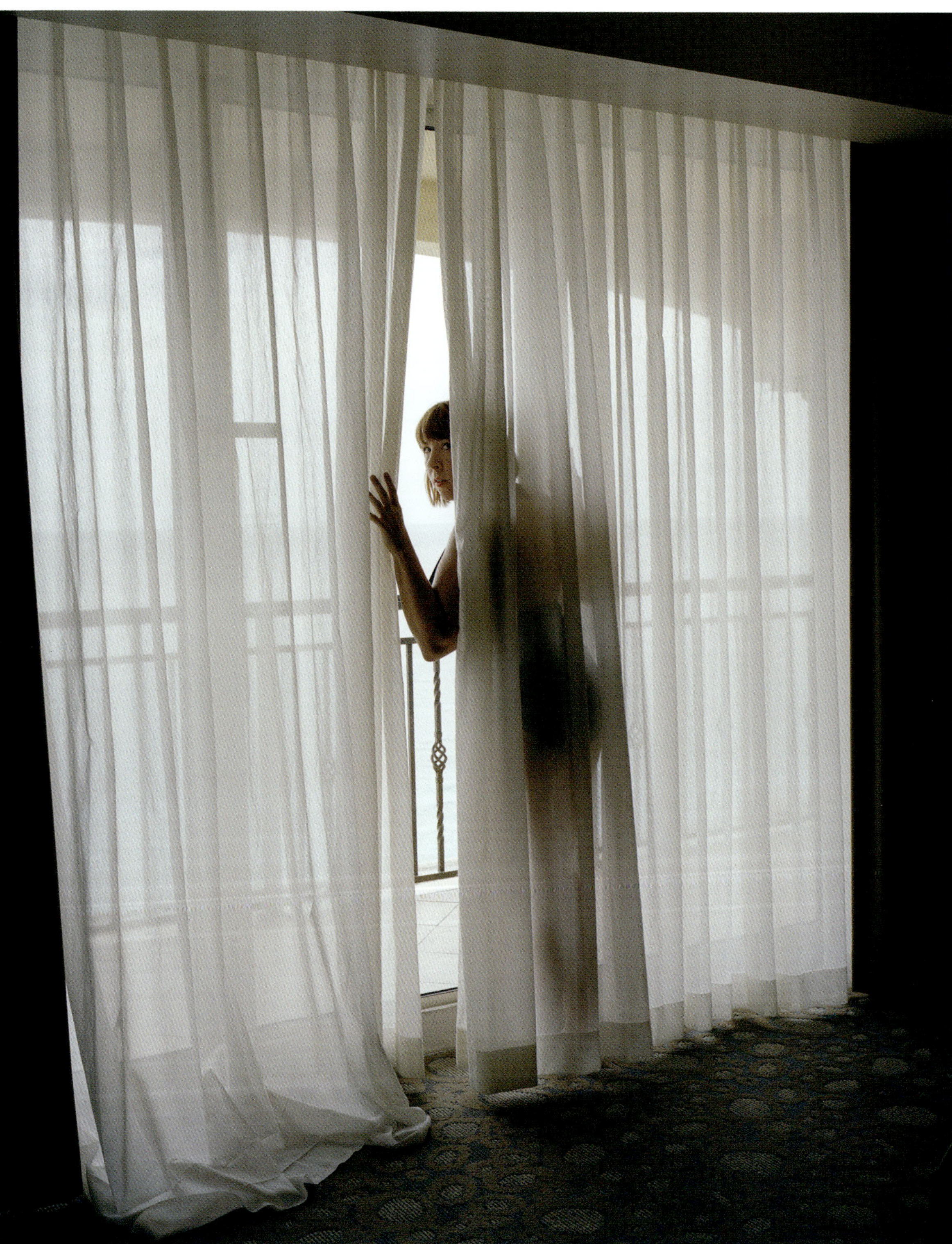

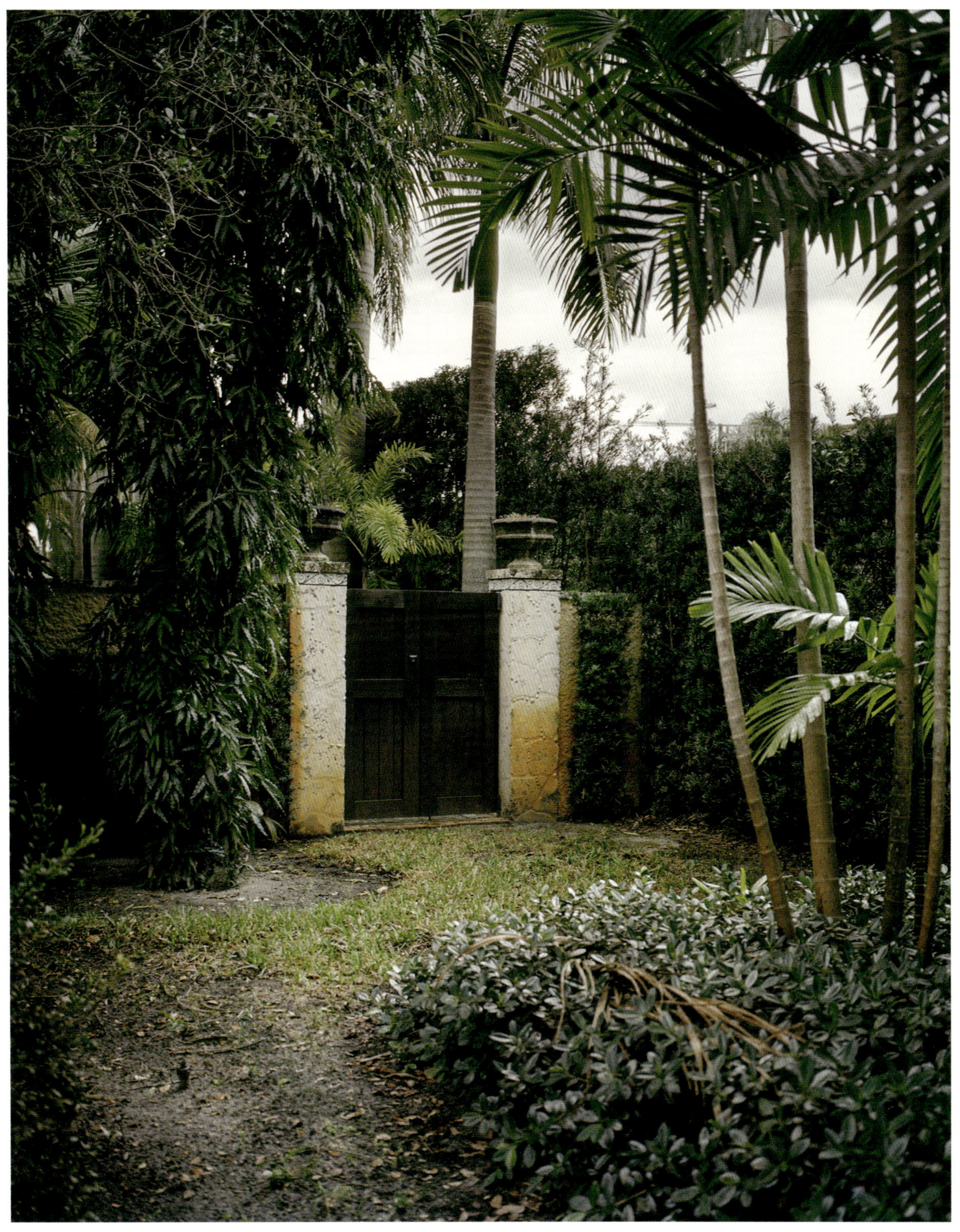

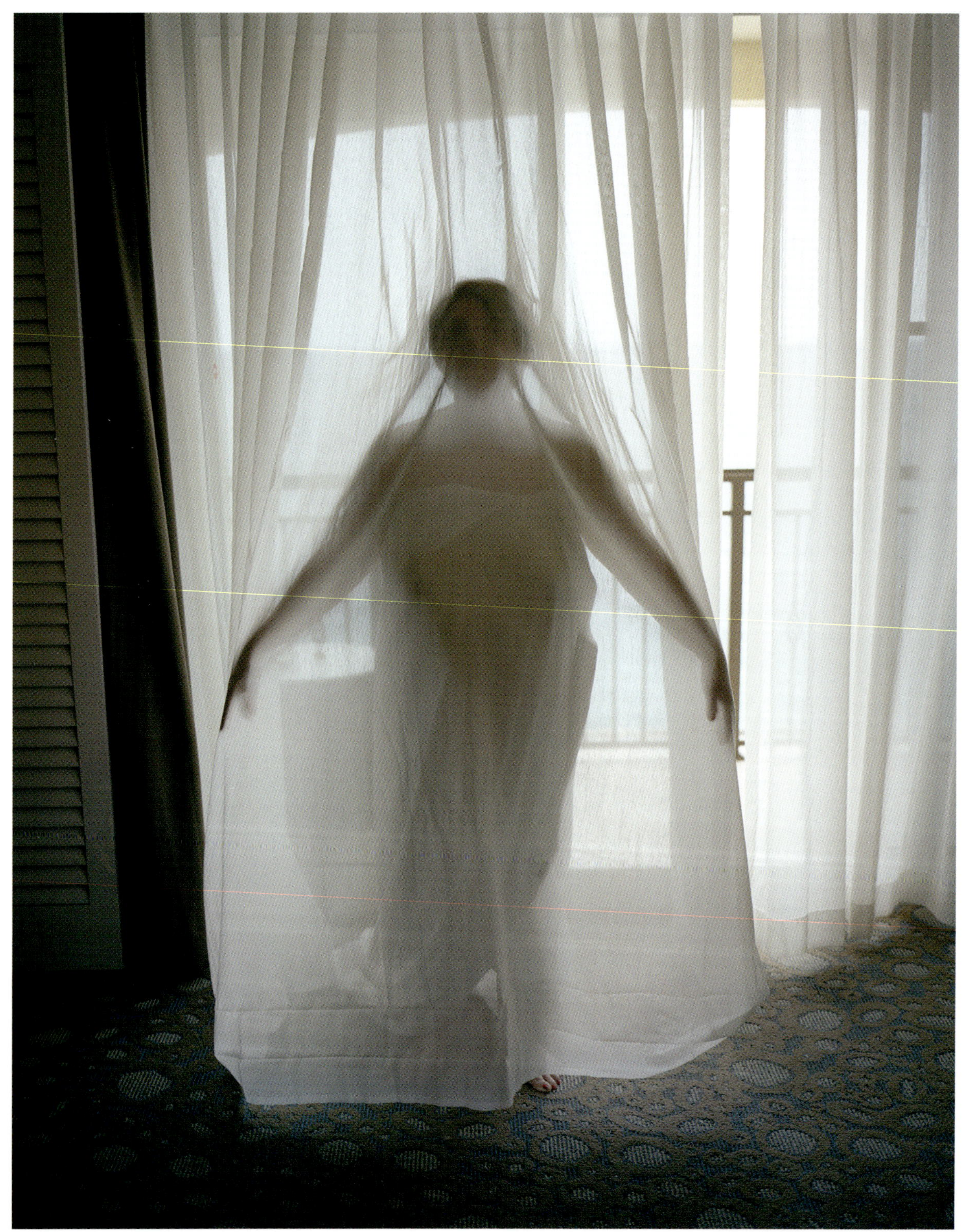

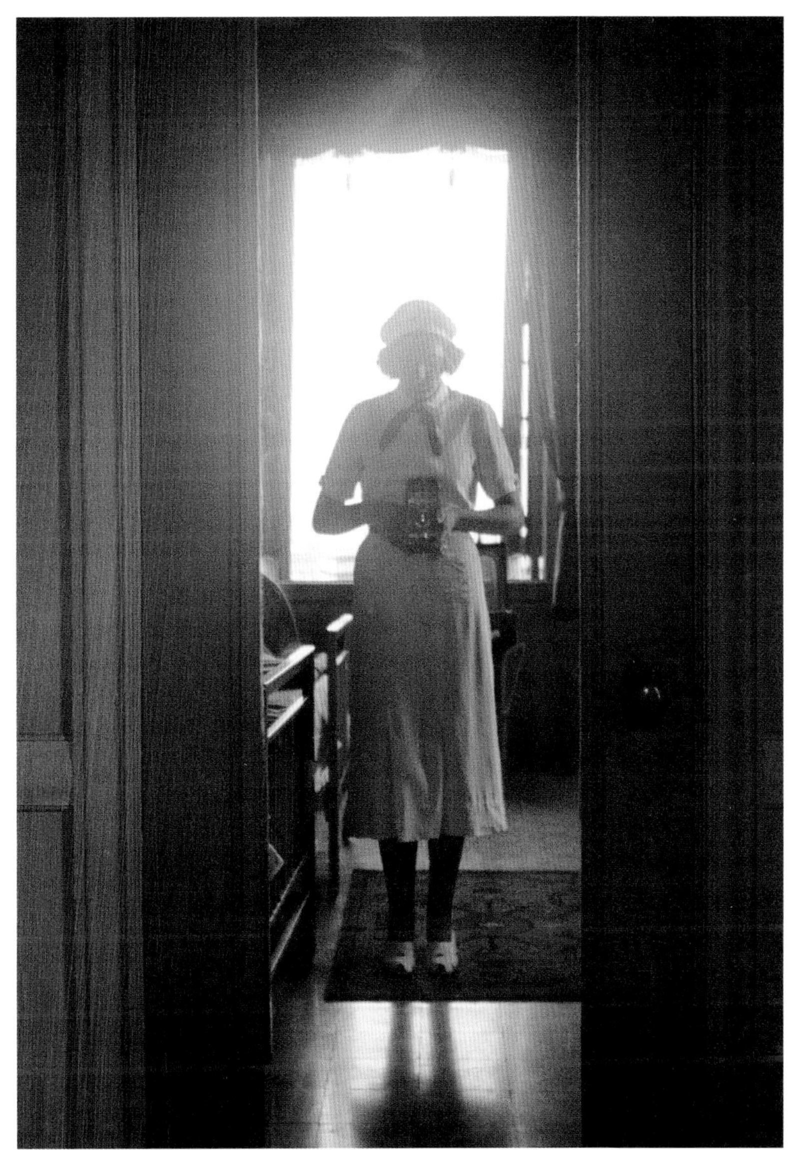

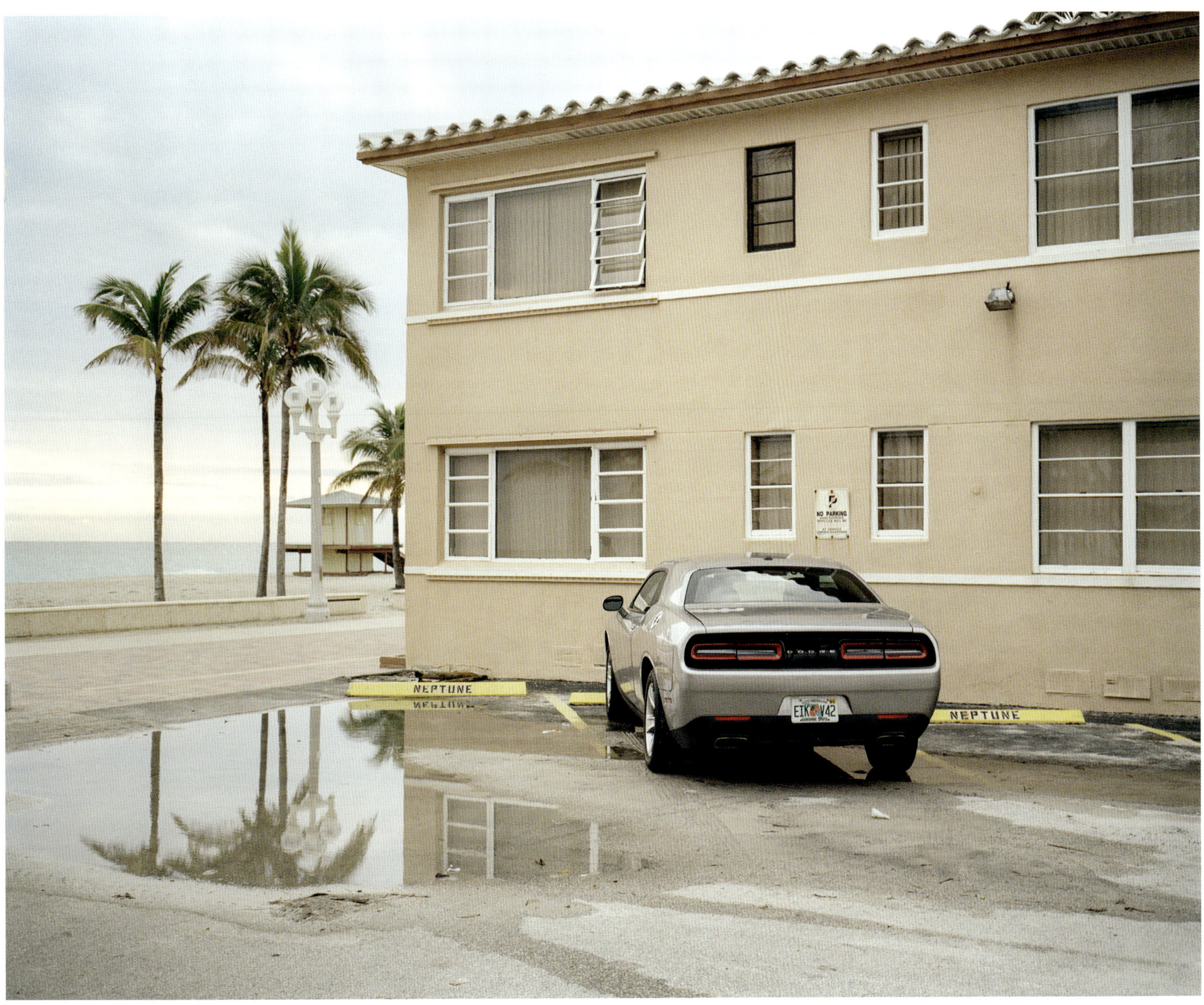
NO PARKING
NEPTUNE
NEPTUNE
NEPTUNE
DODGE
EIK V42

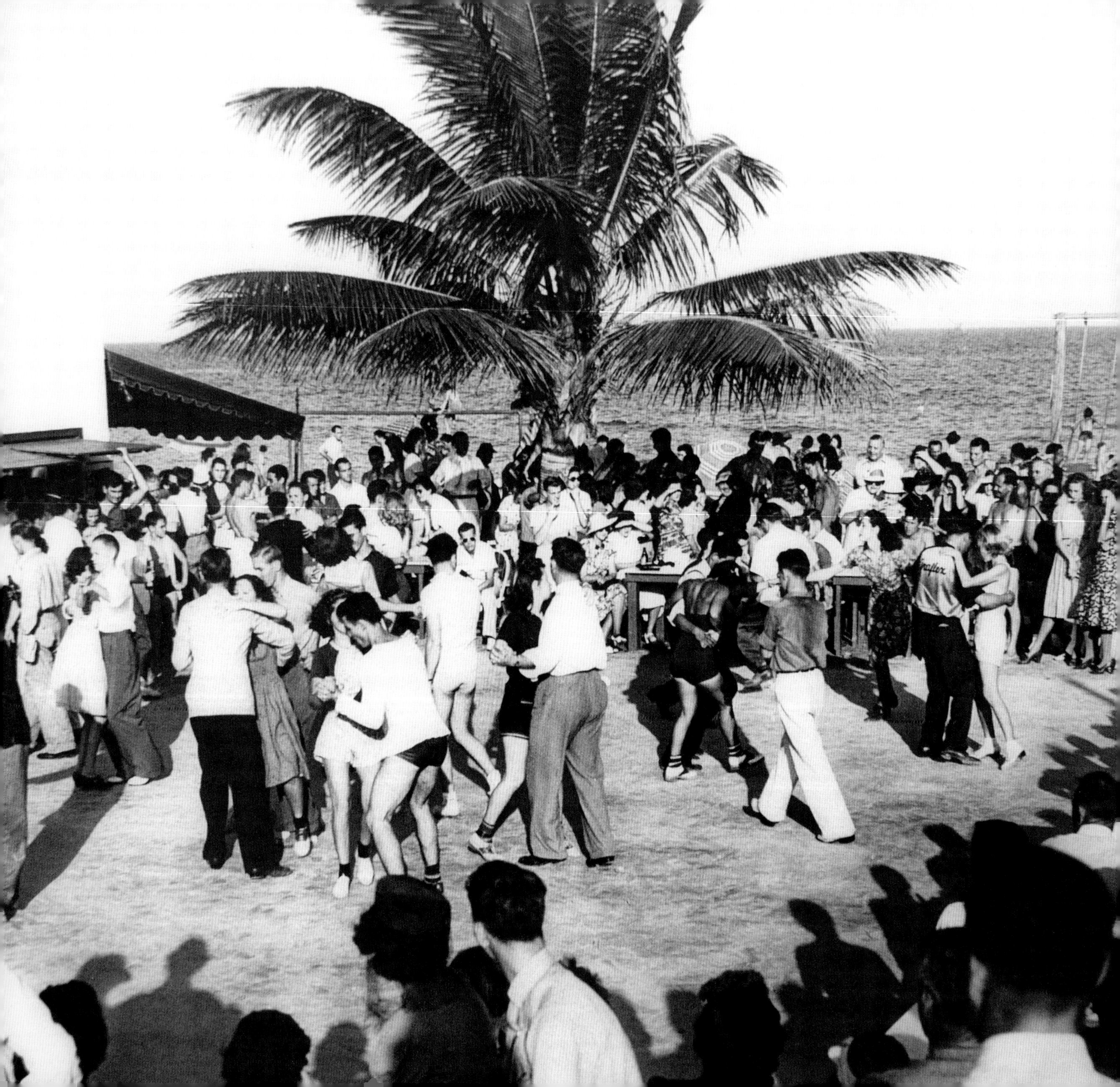

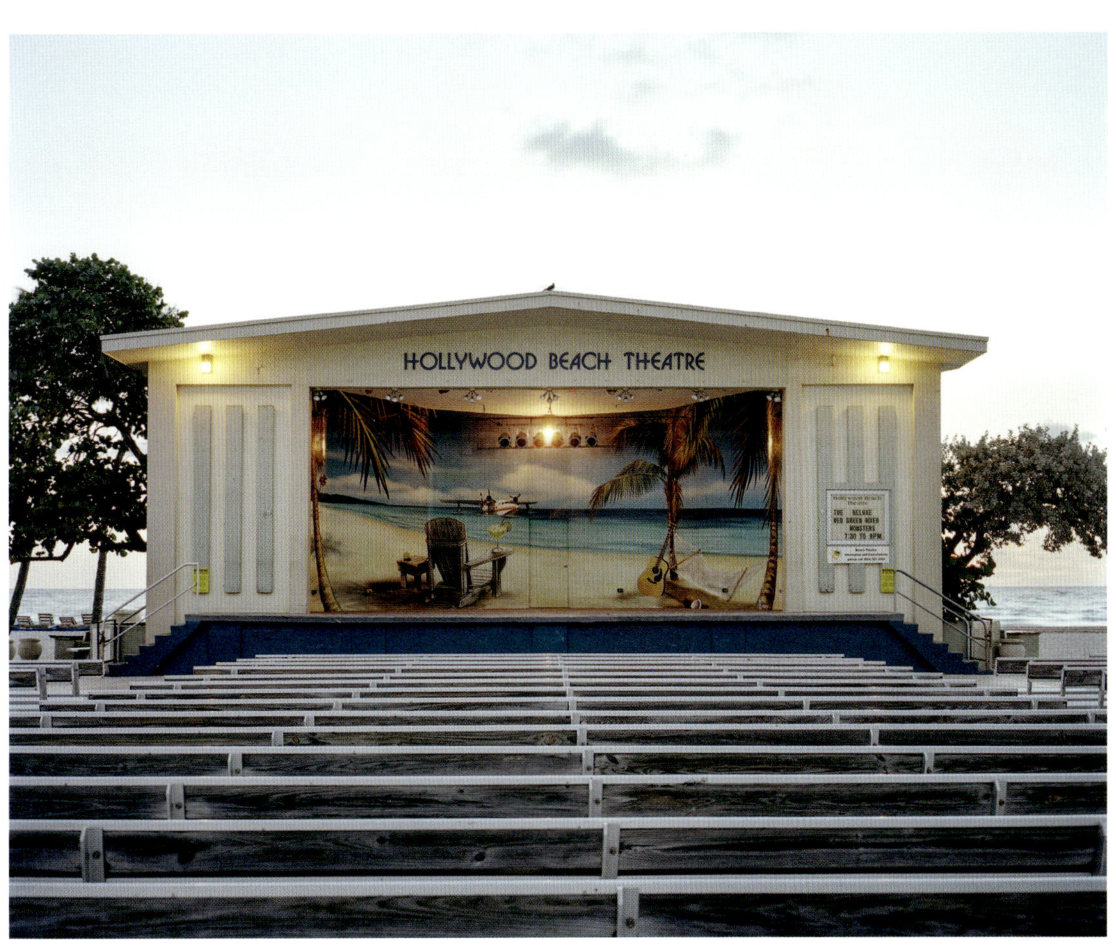

HOLLYWOOD BEACH THEATRE
THE DELUXE
RED GREEN RIVER
MONSTERS
7:30 TO 8PM

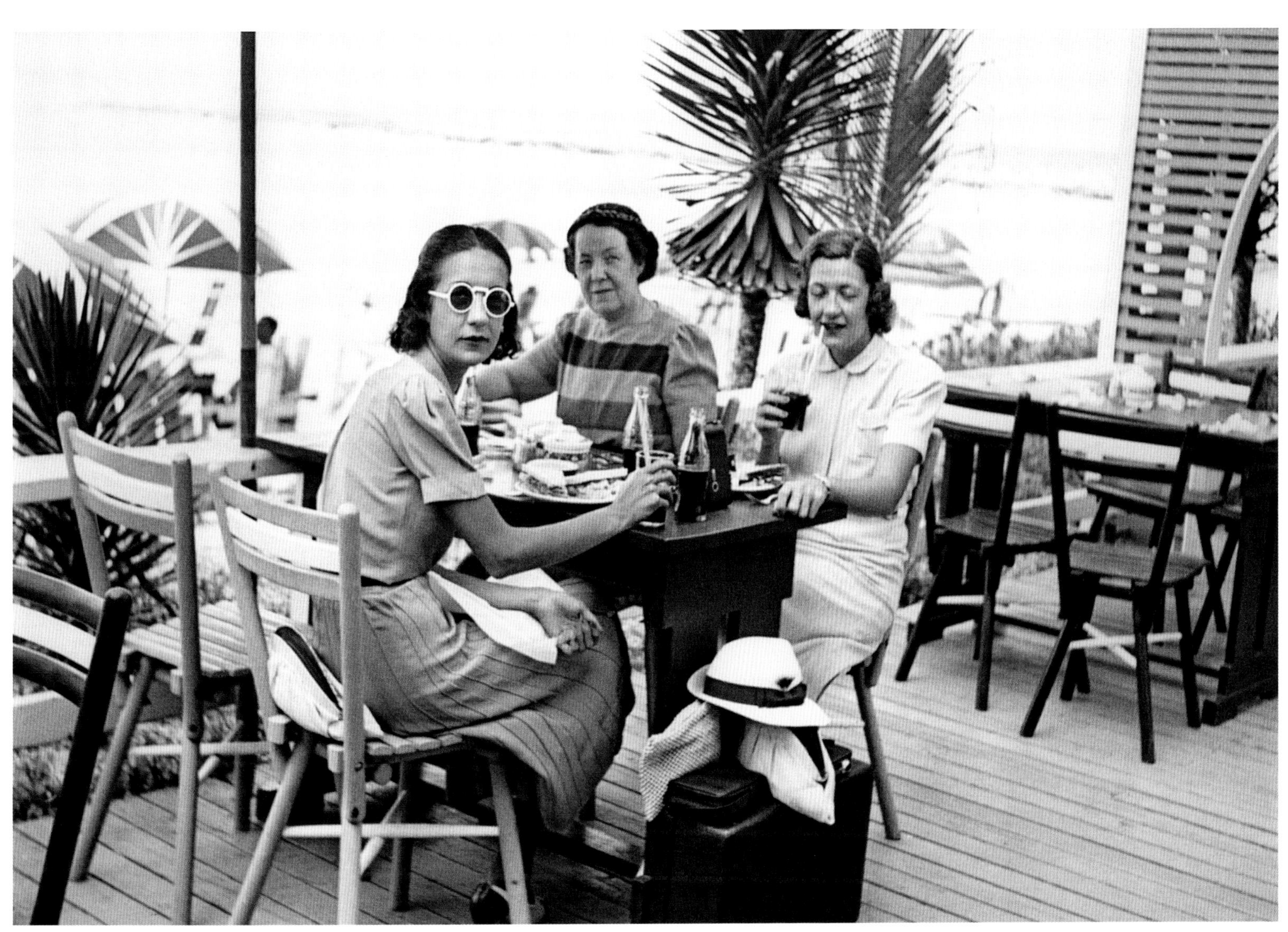

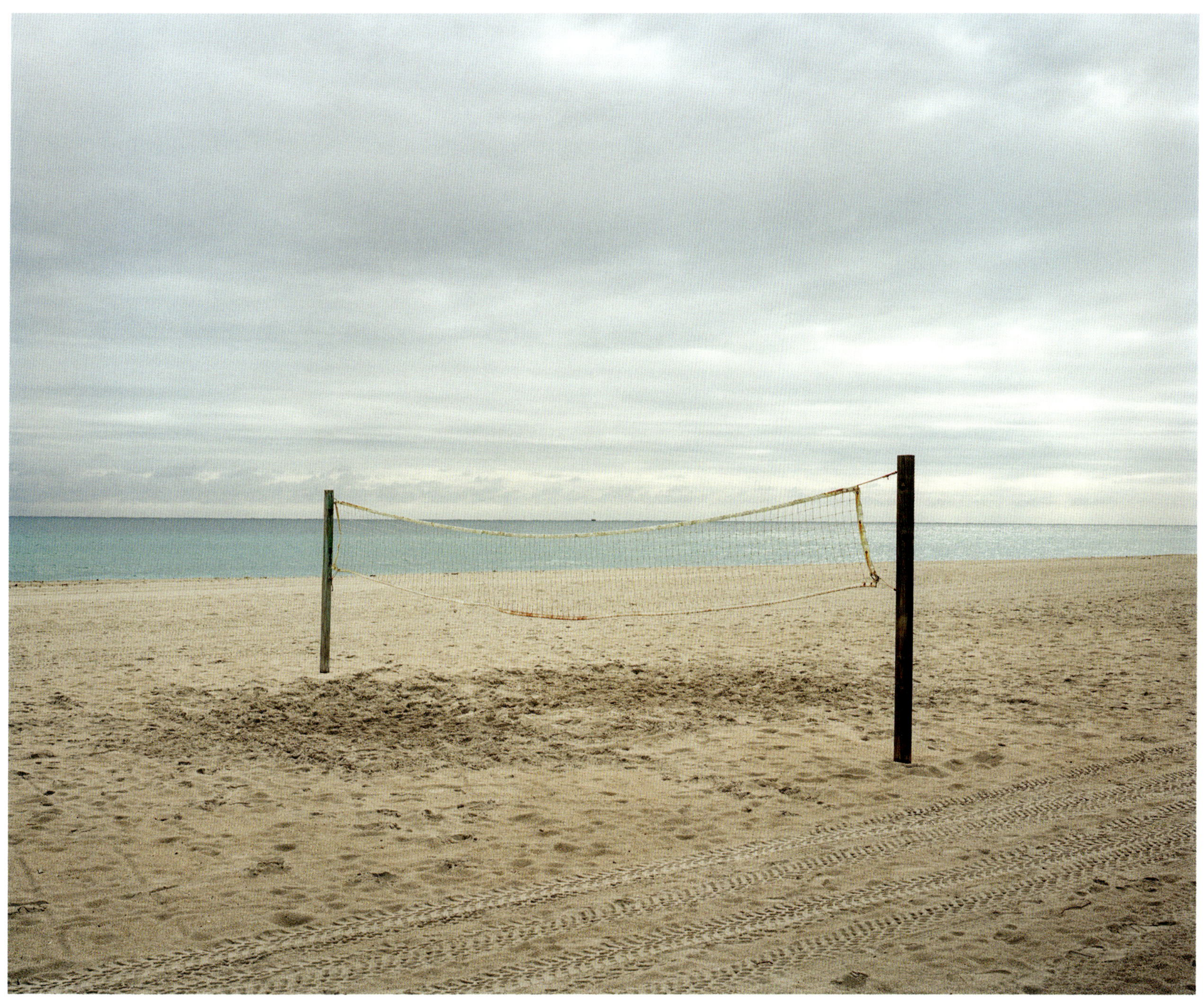

Sun. June 25, 1944.
Houston Texas.
154th Letter.

My Darling Companion,
Another day has come to a close
--- a lot of fun, but ah! have I wished
for Eddie. I'll start from the beginning
and give you some details.

Helen got off here about 10:20 —
we came home soon afterwards.
Naturally, we had a certain amount
to say but saved a lot of it until
"later." We got to sleep about 1:15 — I guess.

Then up at 6:00 this morning —
Some of the members of our church
(about 12) were to sing over "The Voice of the Church."
Bud & Helen went with me. We got there
50 mins. early — we talked to Ivan
Cooksie (? spelling), Charlie Hart — fooled
around — later rehearsed.

We broadcasted at 8:00 — 8:30.
Oh! Guess what Charlie Hart did —
he said (over the air) "It's good to
see Al Haubald, a former op'r, in the central
Room. He's home on furlough. We're
glad to have Mrs. Ed Bost to sing
with us this morning. Her husband,
who is one of our former operator, is some-
where in India — — maybe working
on the B-29's." — It was something
to that effect — it took & me
by surprise — — — everyone looked

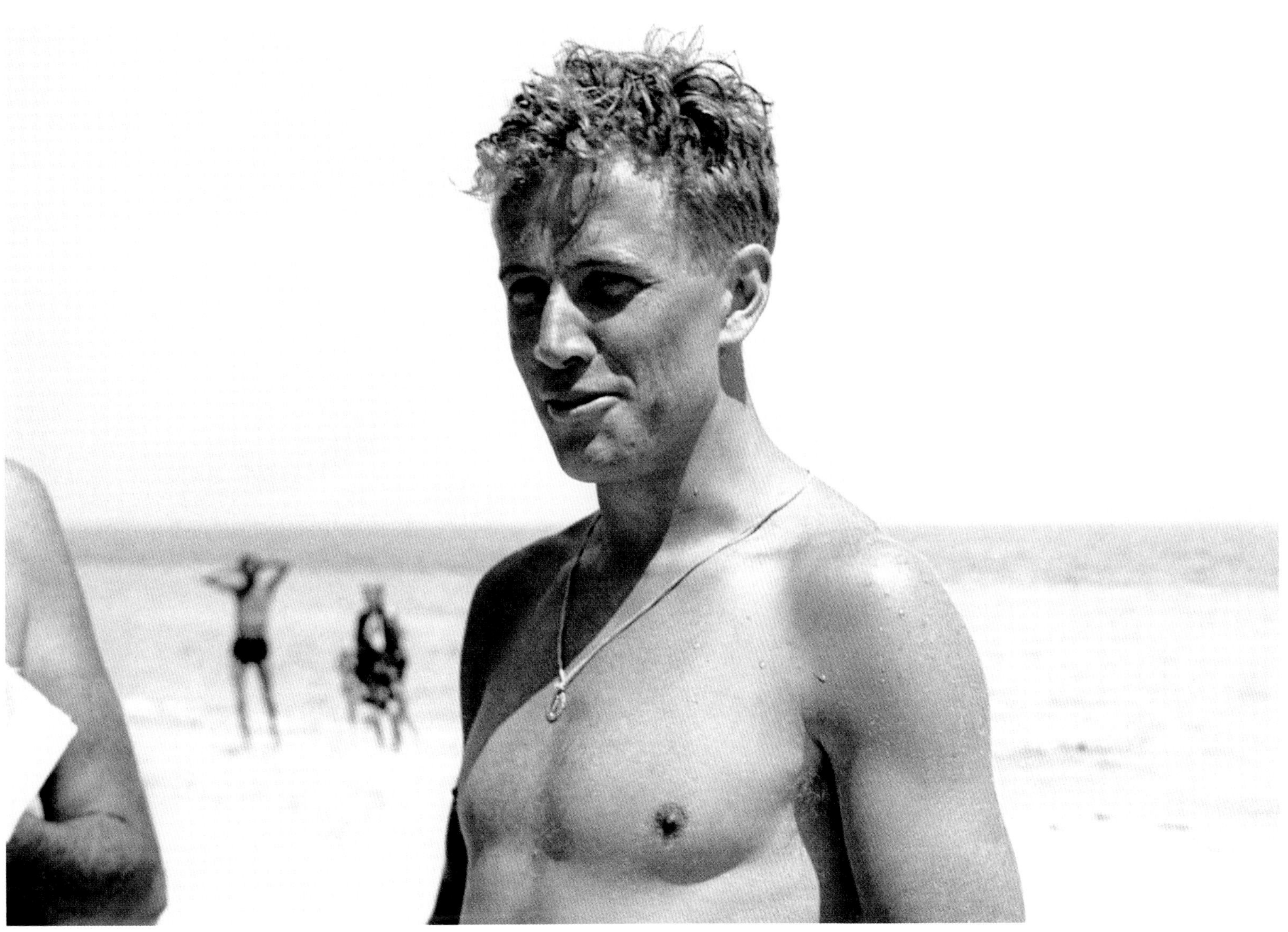

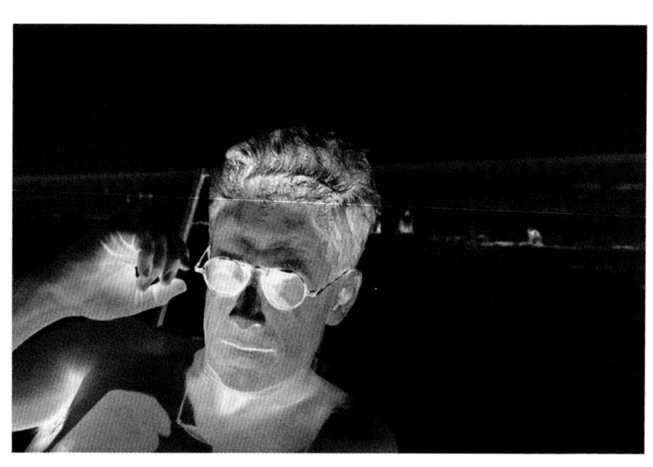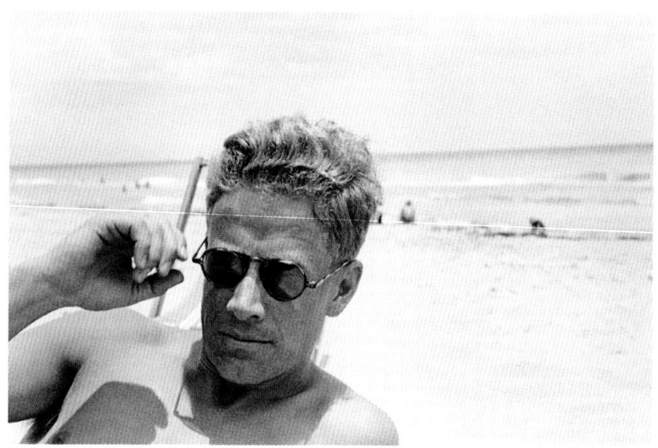

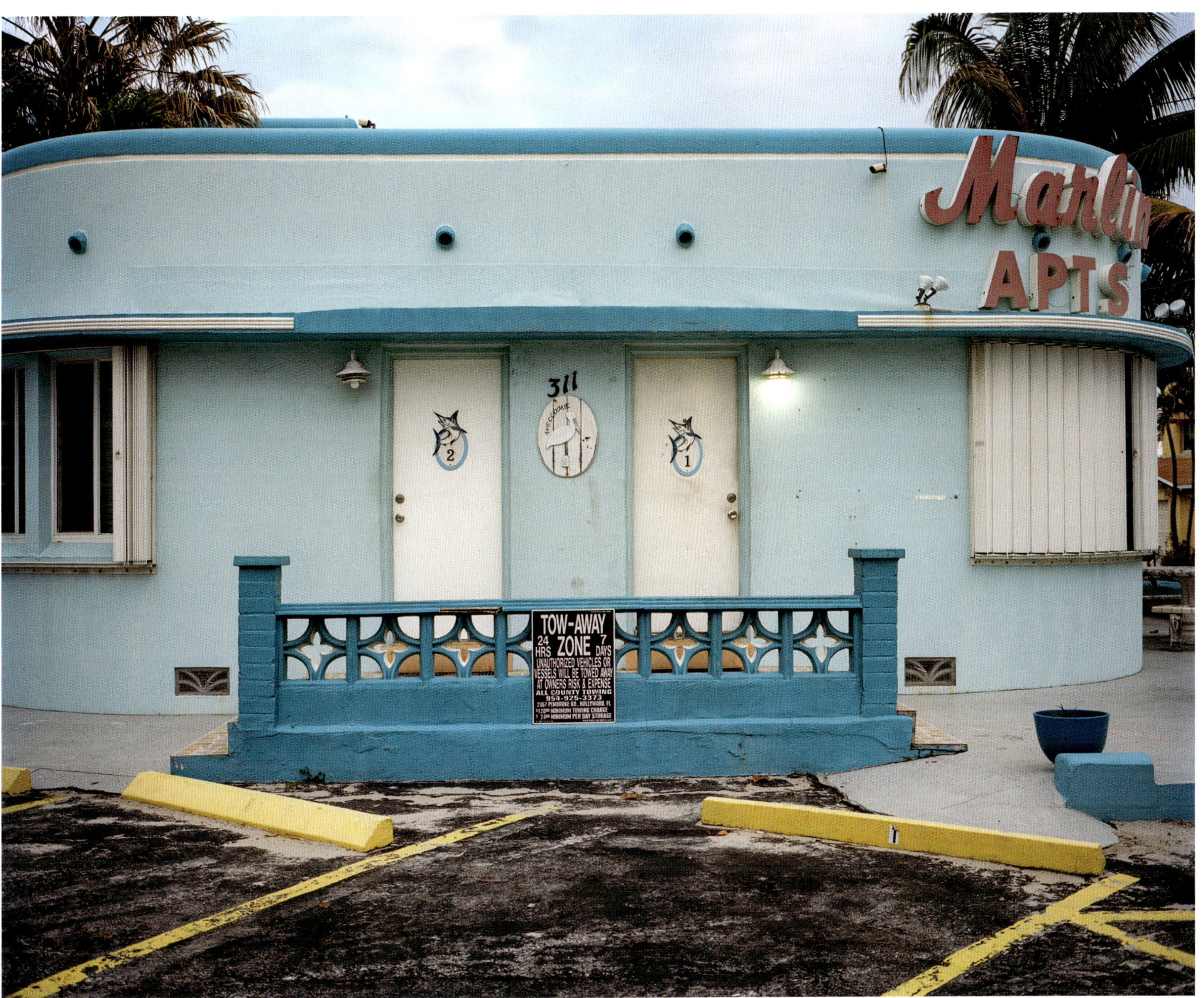

Marlin
APTS
311
TOW-AWAY
24 HRS ZONE 7 DAYS
UNAUTHORIZED VEHICLES OR
VESSELS WILL BE TOWED AWAY
AT OWNERS RISK & EXPENSE
ALL COUNTY TOWING
954-925-3373

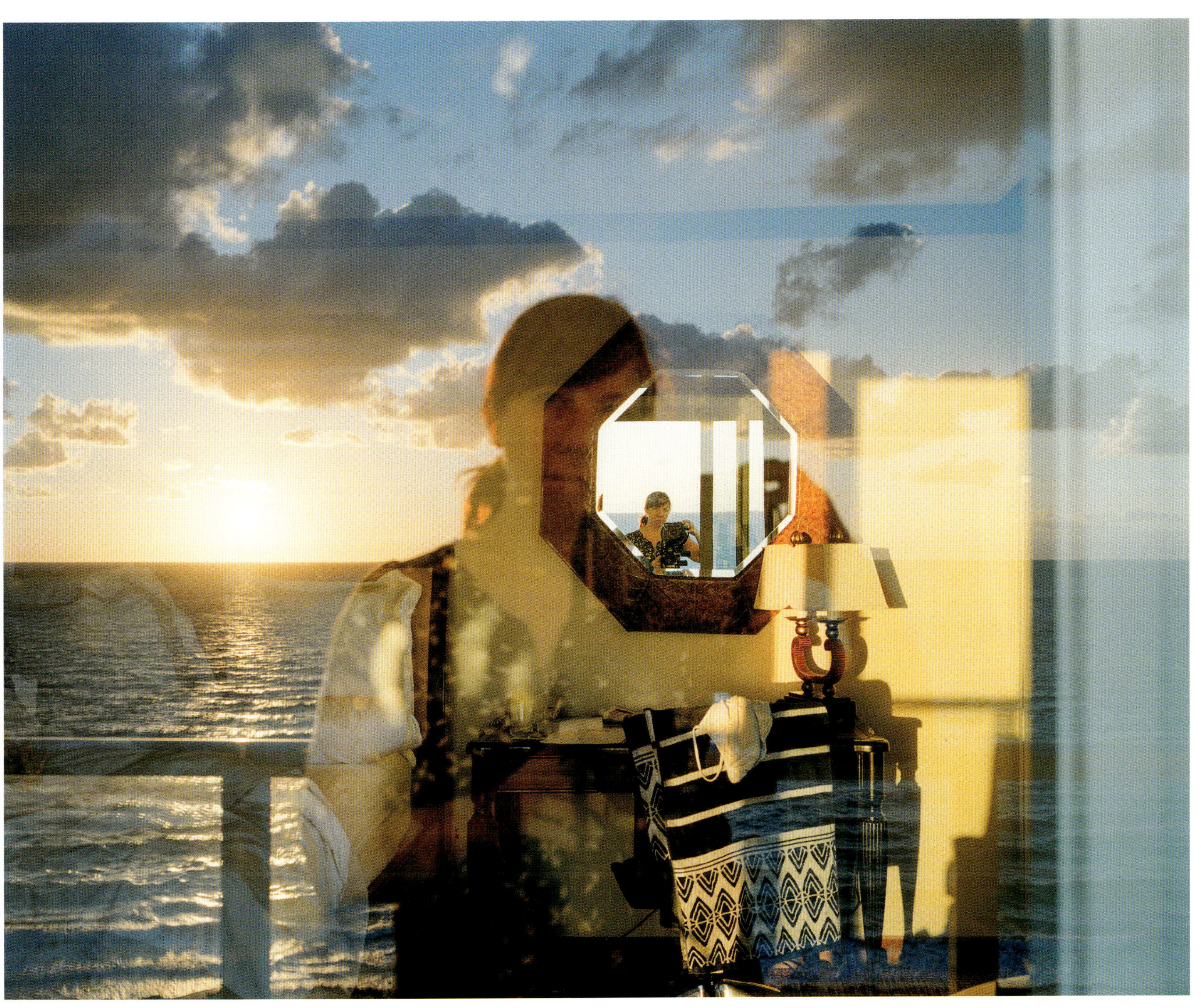

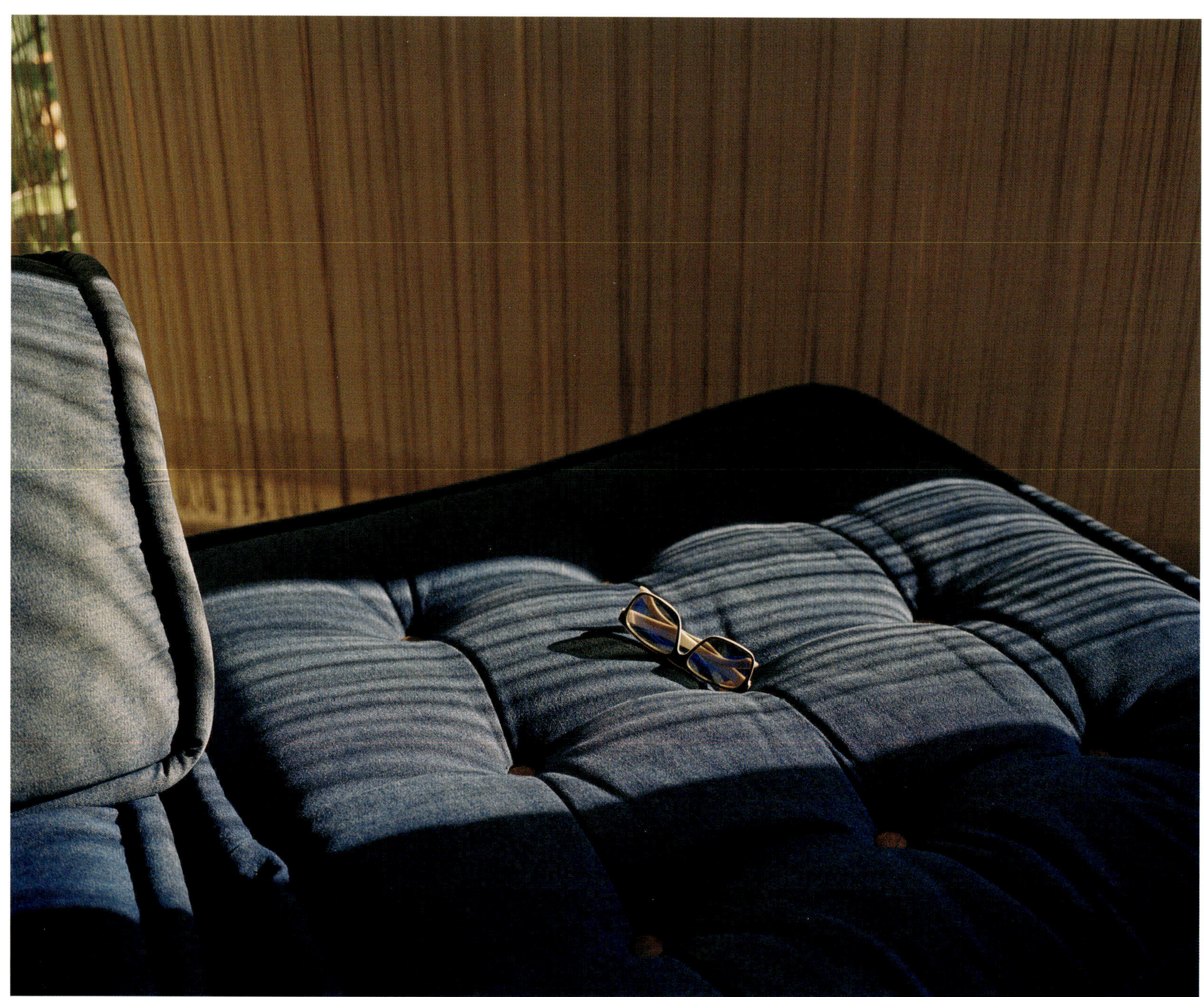

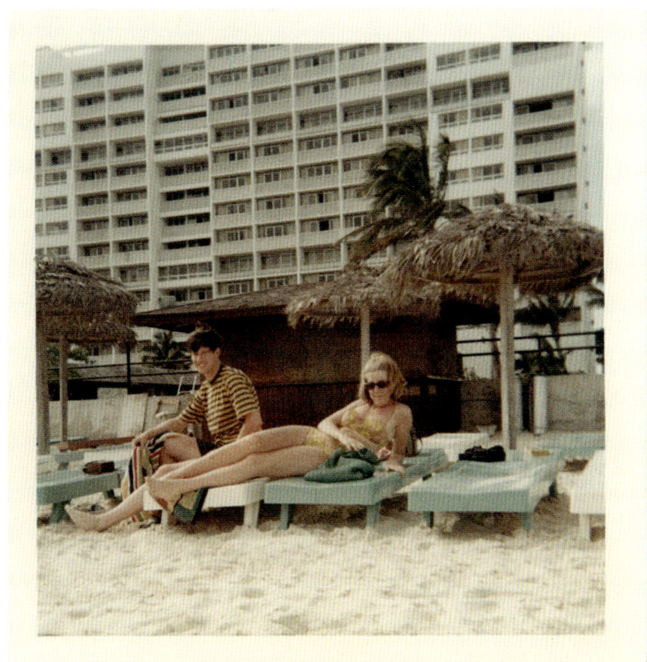

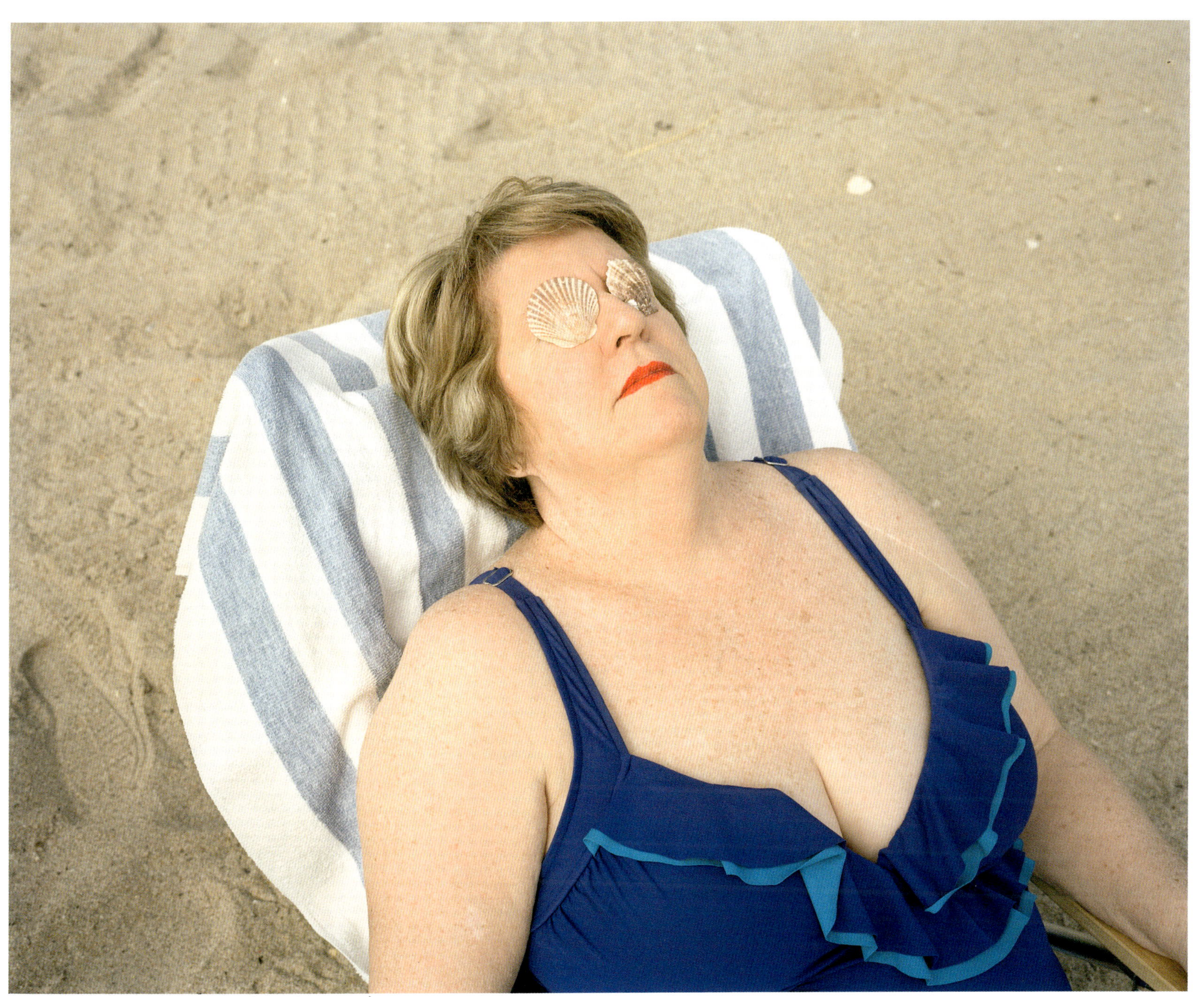

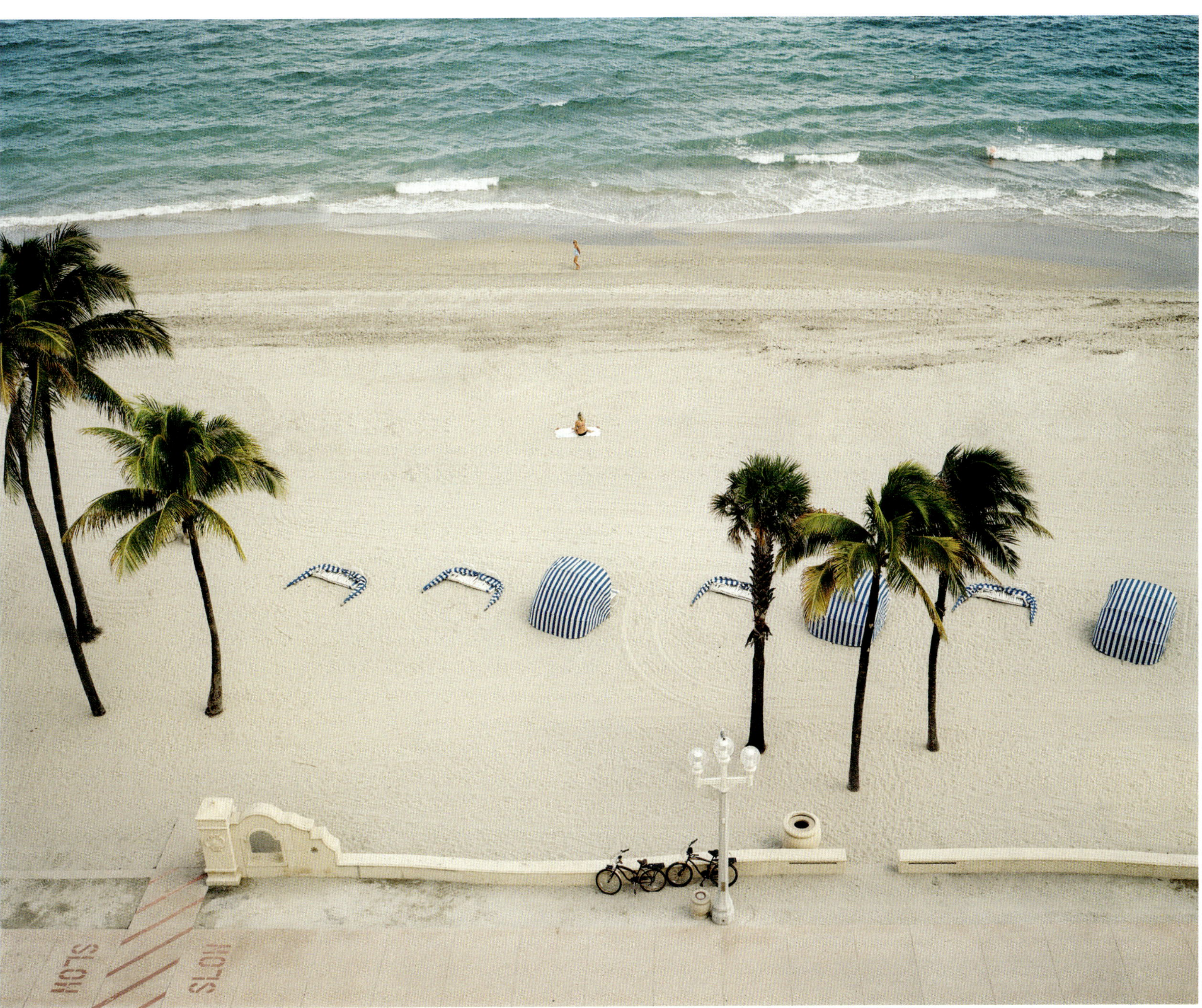
SLOW
SLOW

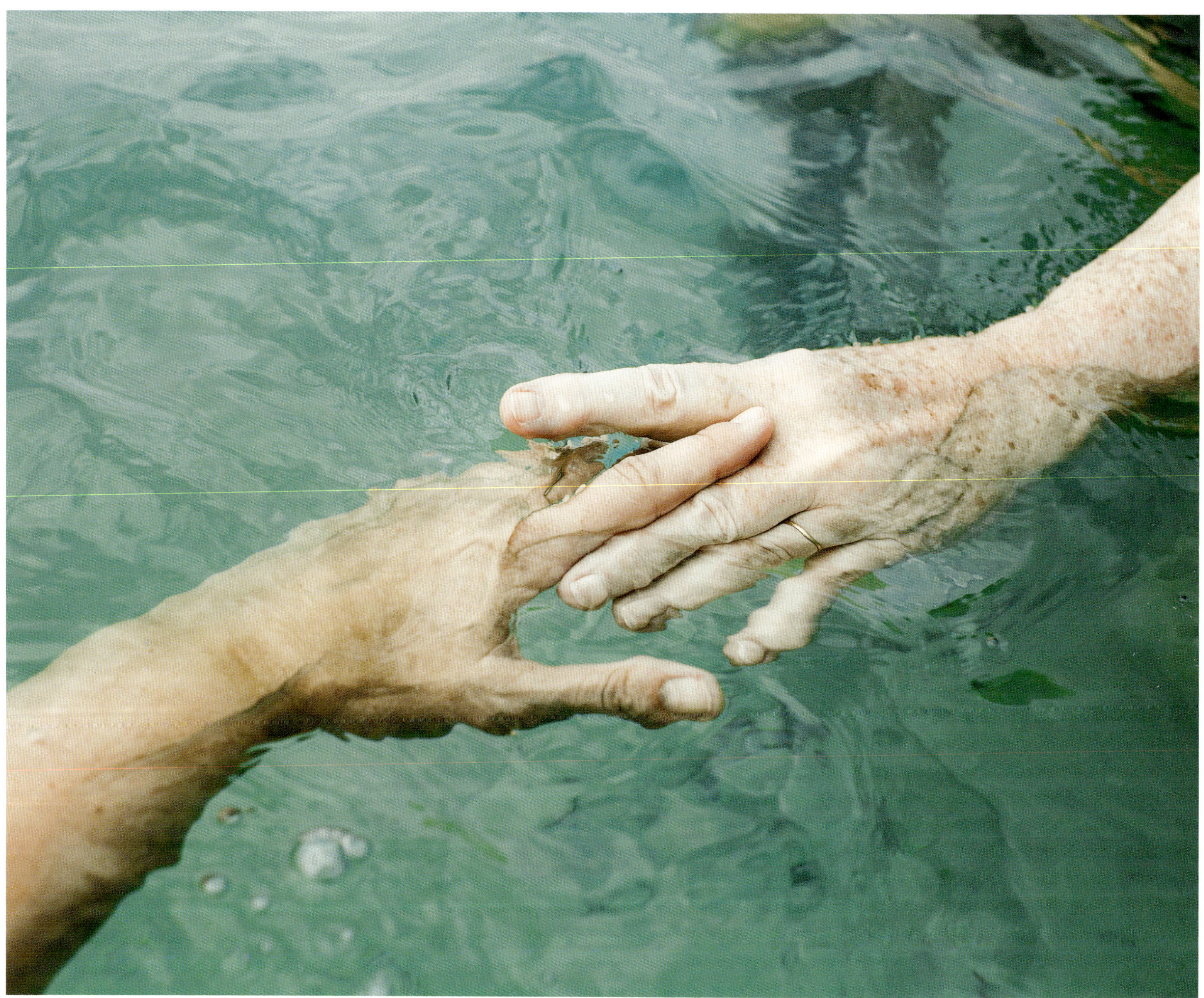

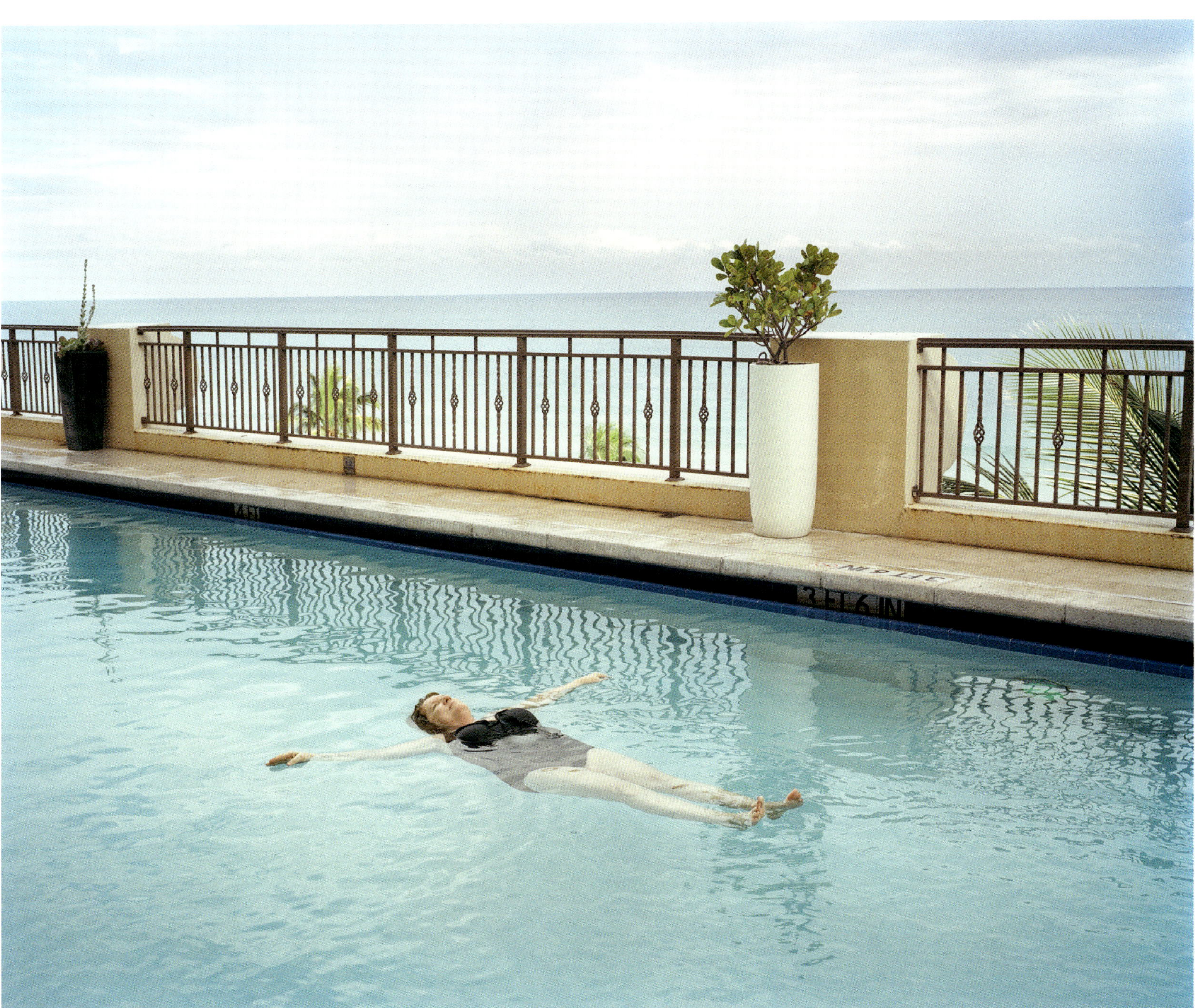

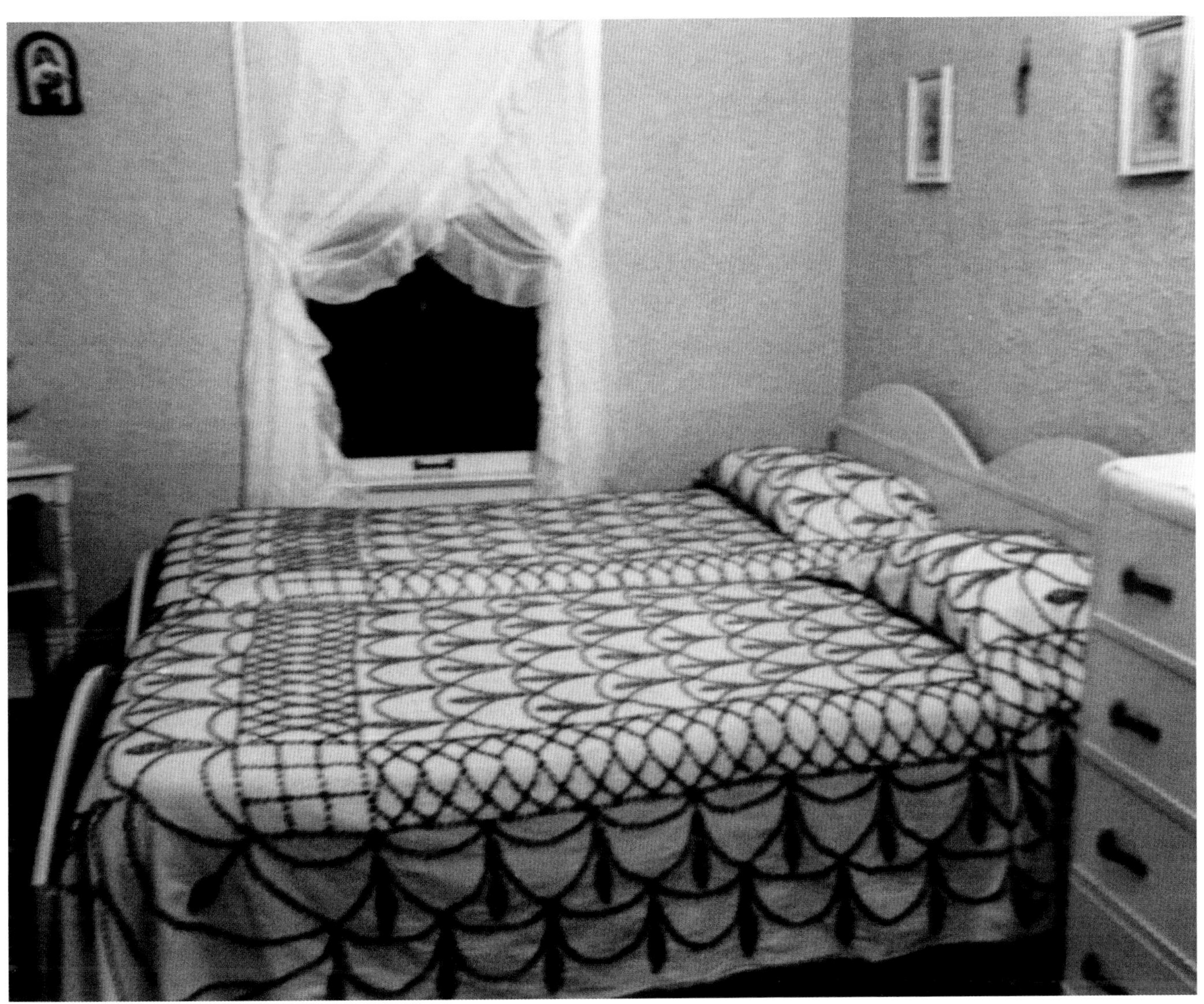

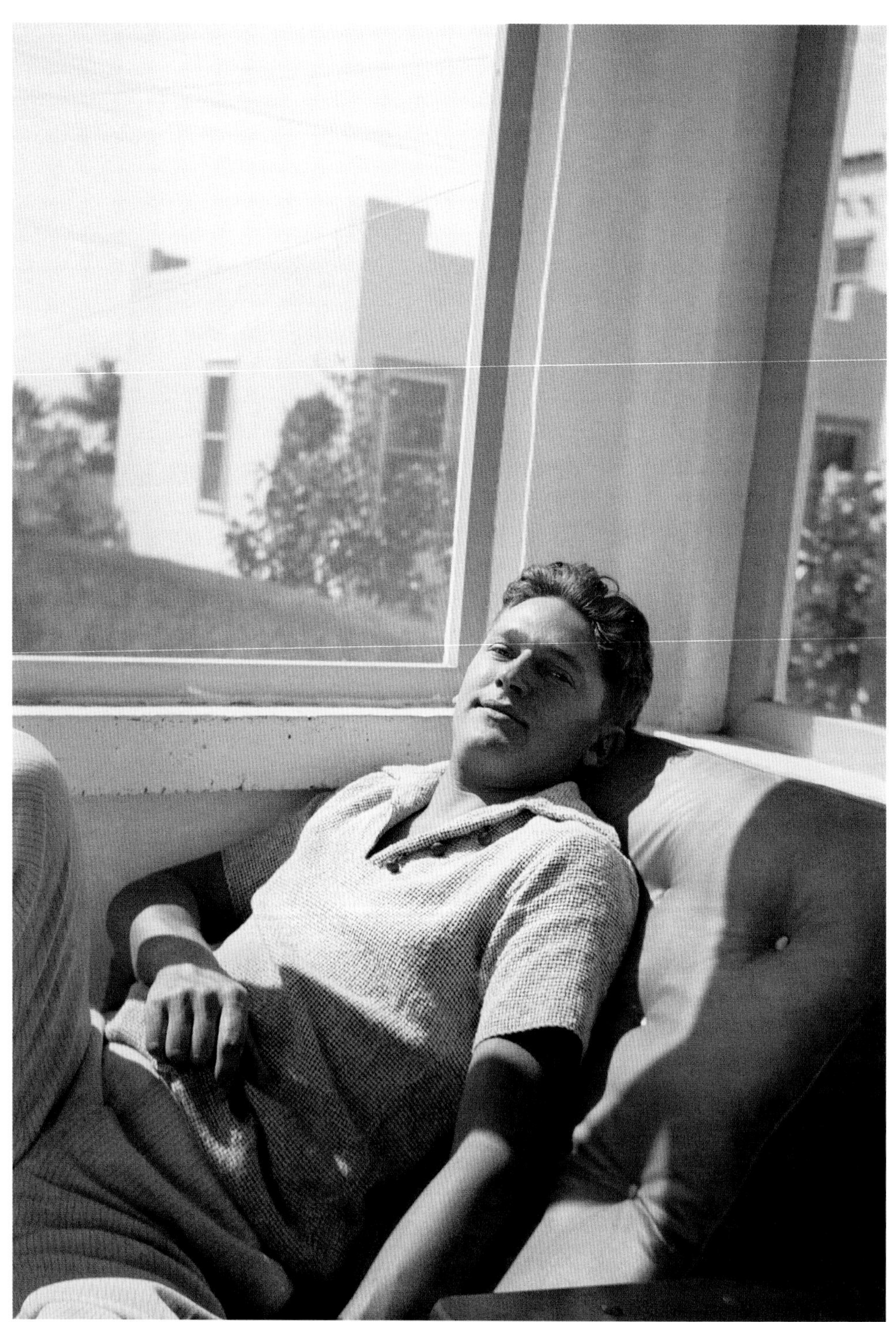

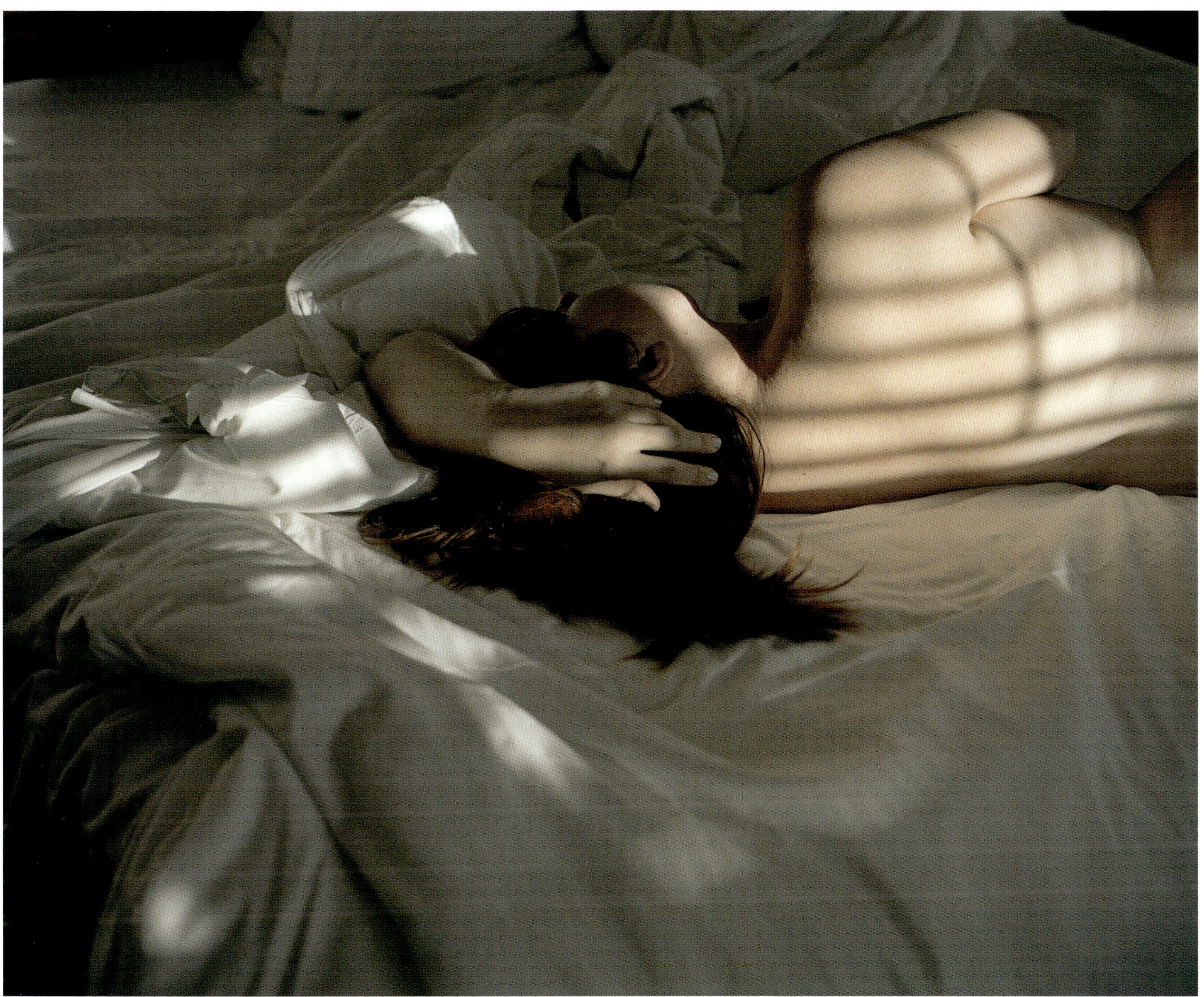

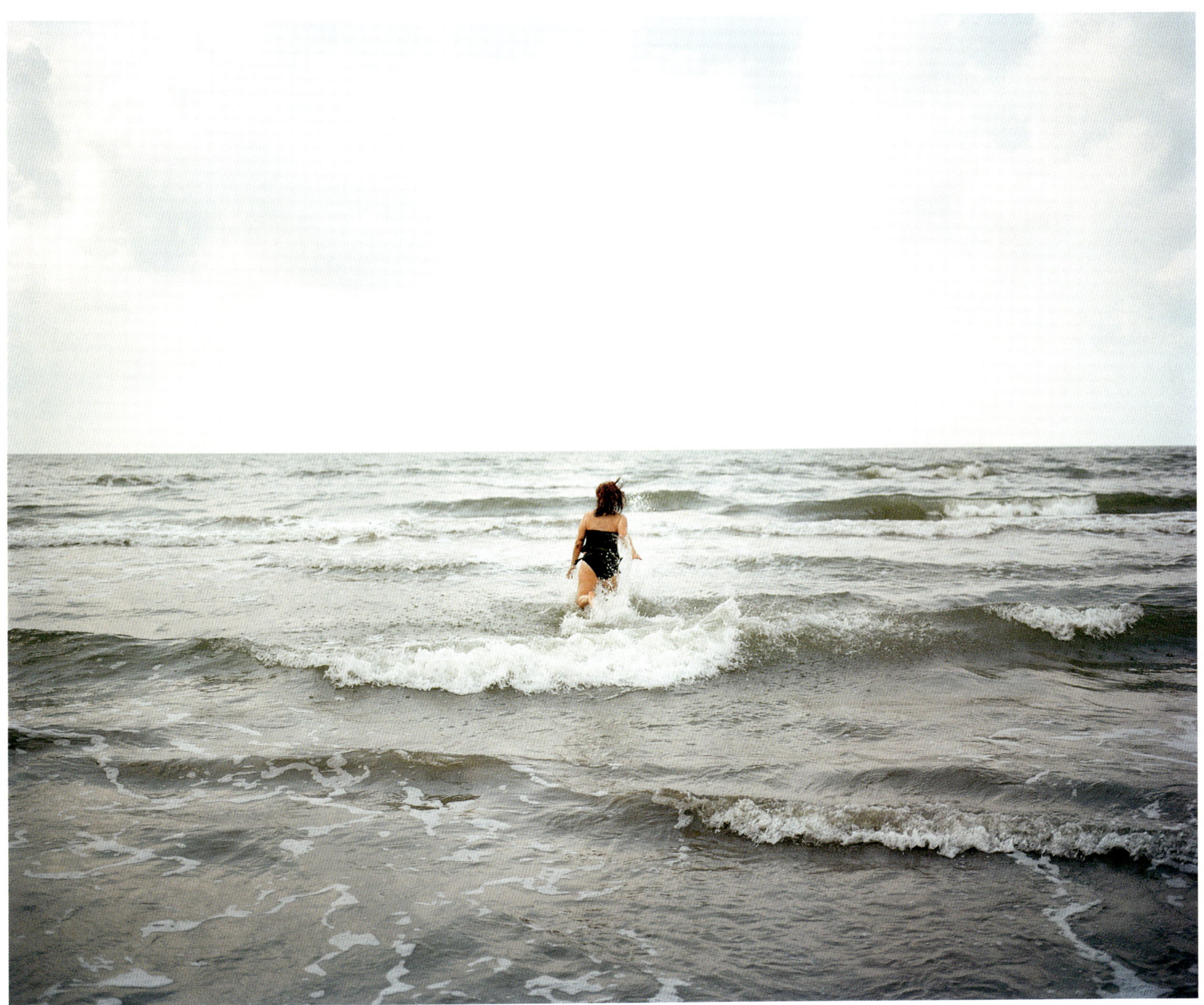

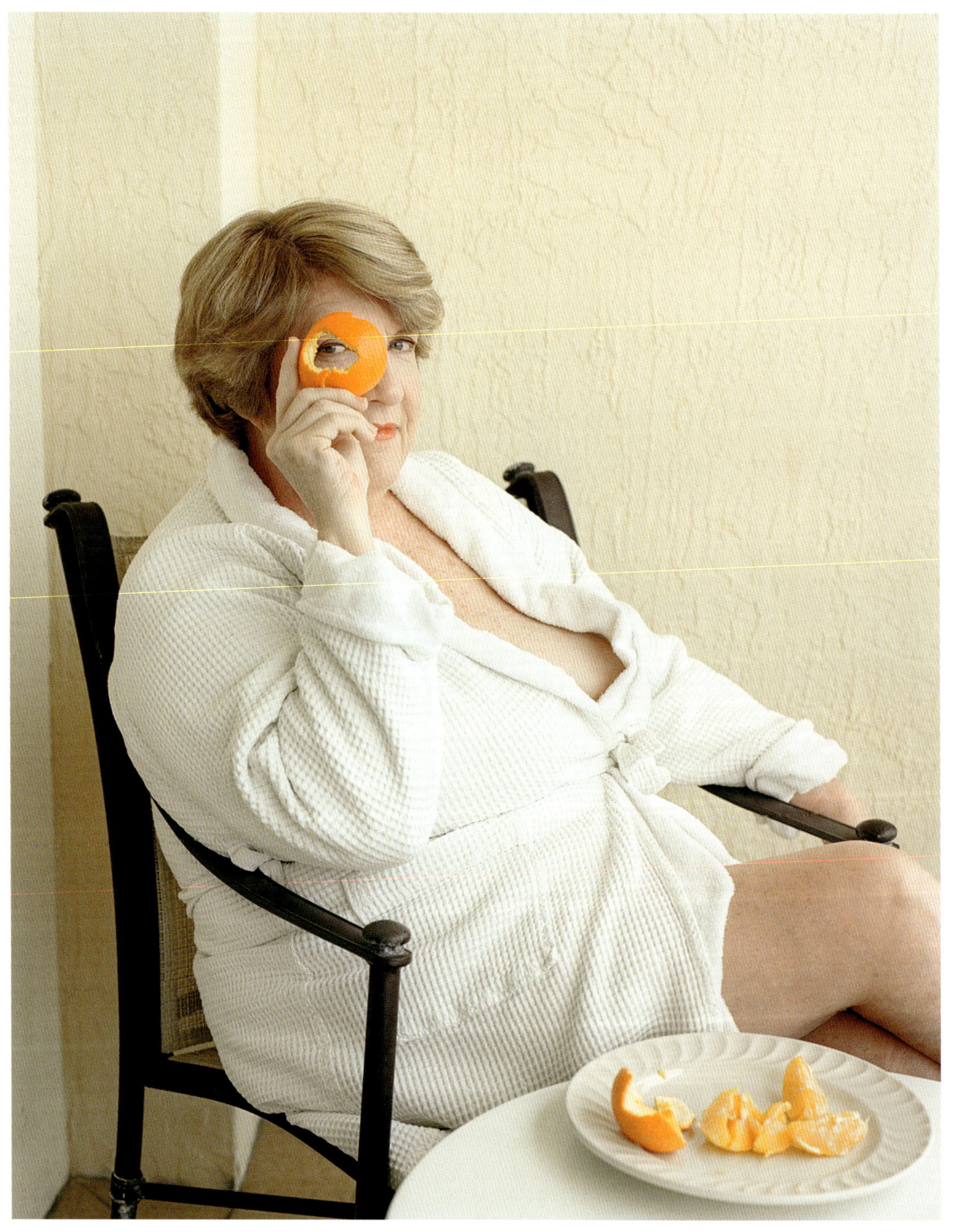

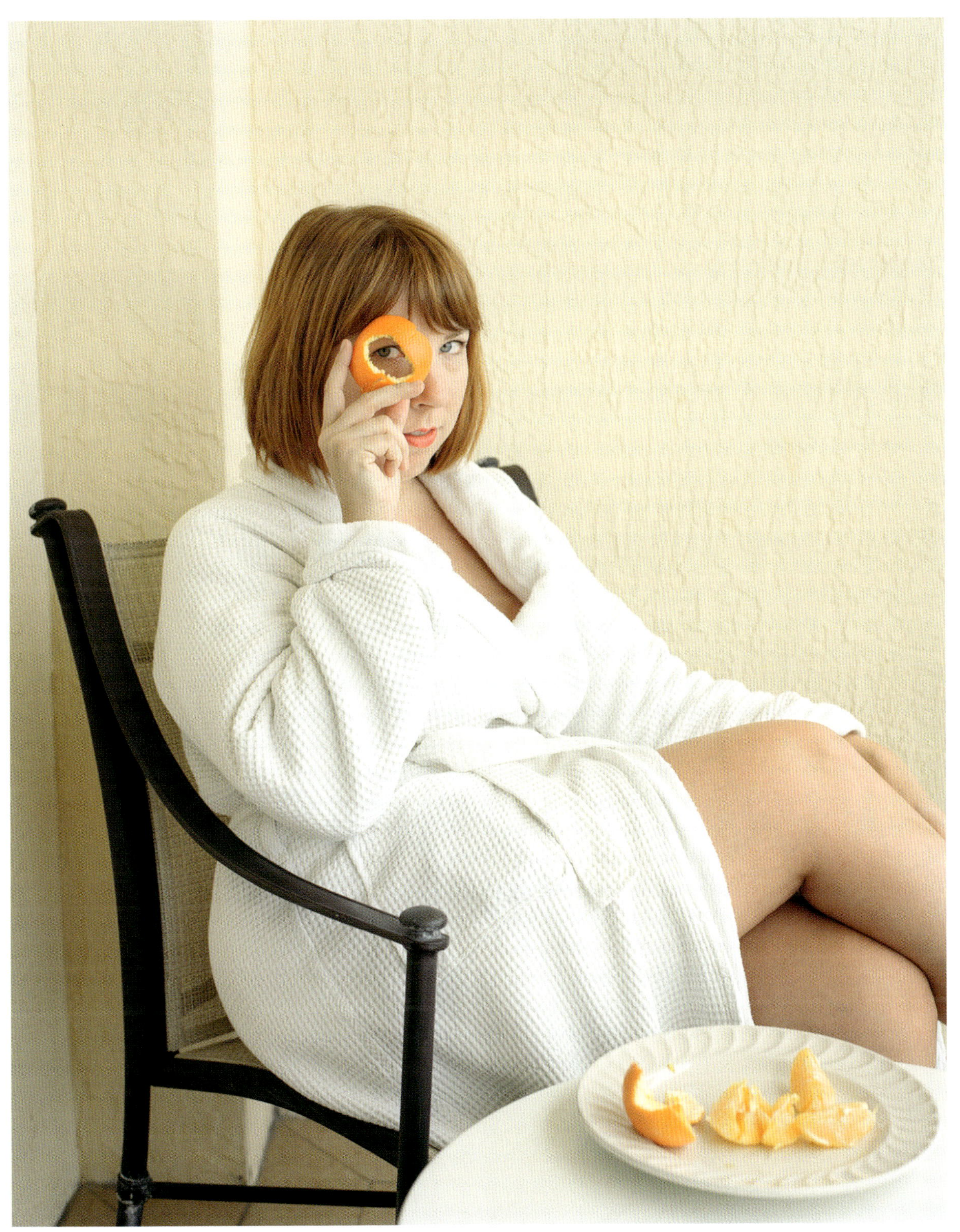

I feel like I'm writing a composition! Well, anyway, I
went down to Florida with four guys and five girls (including
me). The drive to miami took 23 hours, and it was quite an un-
comfortable trip. But the country is so pretty on the drive down.
I had never seen most of it before, so I stayed awake most of the
time and looked out the window.

We got to our hotel at about 8:30 and it was pouring rain.
We were all so depressed and tired that we unpacked and went to
sleep until 5 P.M. Four girls in two single beds — sardines!

The next day, we all went down to the beach, boys too.
It was a beautiful day. We met the kids from North East Illinois
Univ. (Chicago) and they invited us to a beach party that night.
I met John. He's 6'2" tall, brown hair and a mustache; he's
really great and we had a good time together.

These kids got a room but no meals in their deal with the
hotel, but you should have seen their rooms! All we had was a
bedroom and bath - facing the fromt of the hotel. They had a
livingroom, plus bedroom and bath — and a balcony, with sliding
glass doors, facing the ocean - really tough. Well, this night
was like right out of a story book. A full moon came up over the
ocean, the air was warm and balmy — just picture it — dancing
under the stars on the balcony! Not too cool! I had the time of
my life. John is so smart and mature and mannerly. He really
spoiled me. Older men are so neat! Ha!

Friday John was leaving (Boo Hoo!) but he called up at about
11 A.M. and came over - all decked out in a suit. He brought us
over all the leftover booze that he and his roommate hadn't fini-
shed. Then he took me out to lunch and then to the Inter-
national Bazaar in the middle of the island. It was like a small
world's fair, with beautiful old shops from many countries. We
stopped at this French outdoor cafe and had a drink and he asked
for my address. Then at 3 P.M. we went back and said goodbye in
this gorgeous tropical garden and he got on his bus and left for
the airport. I went out to the pool, where the girls were
swimming. I must have been looking all misty, cause they started
yelling, "Oh no, she's in love again!" Guess I'm not too
obvious, Huh?

It was really a wonderful, memorable trip and we all had
a marvelous time. If you have any questions (I know that parts
of this might be confusing) than just write and ask them.
At any rate, WRITE SOON.

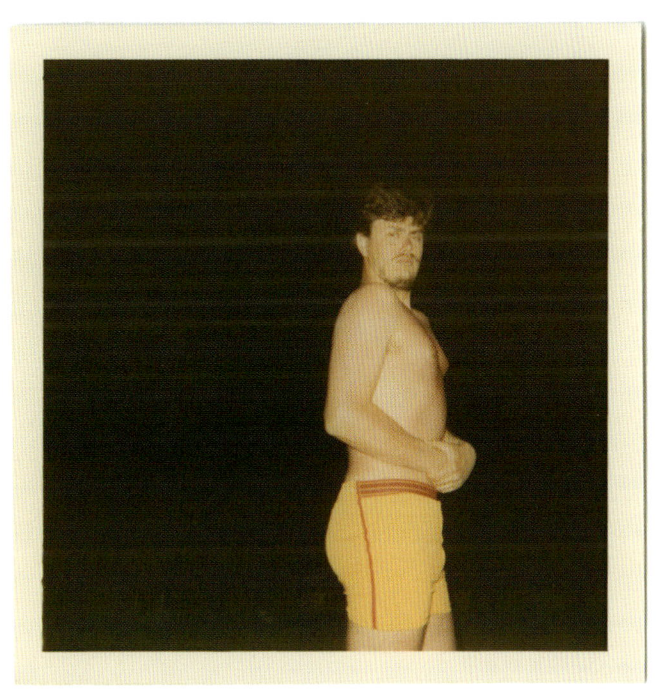

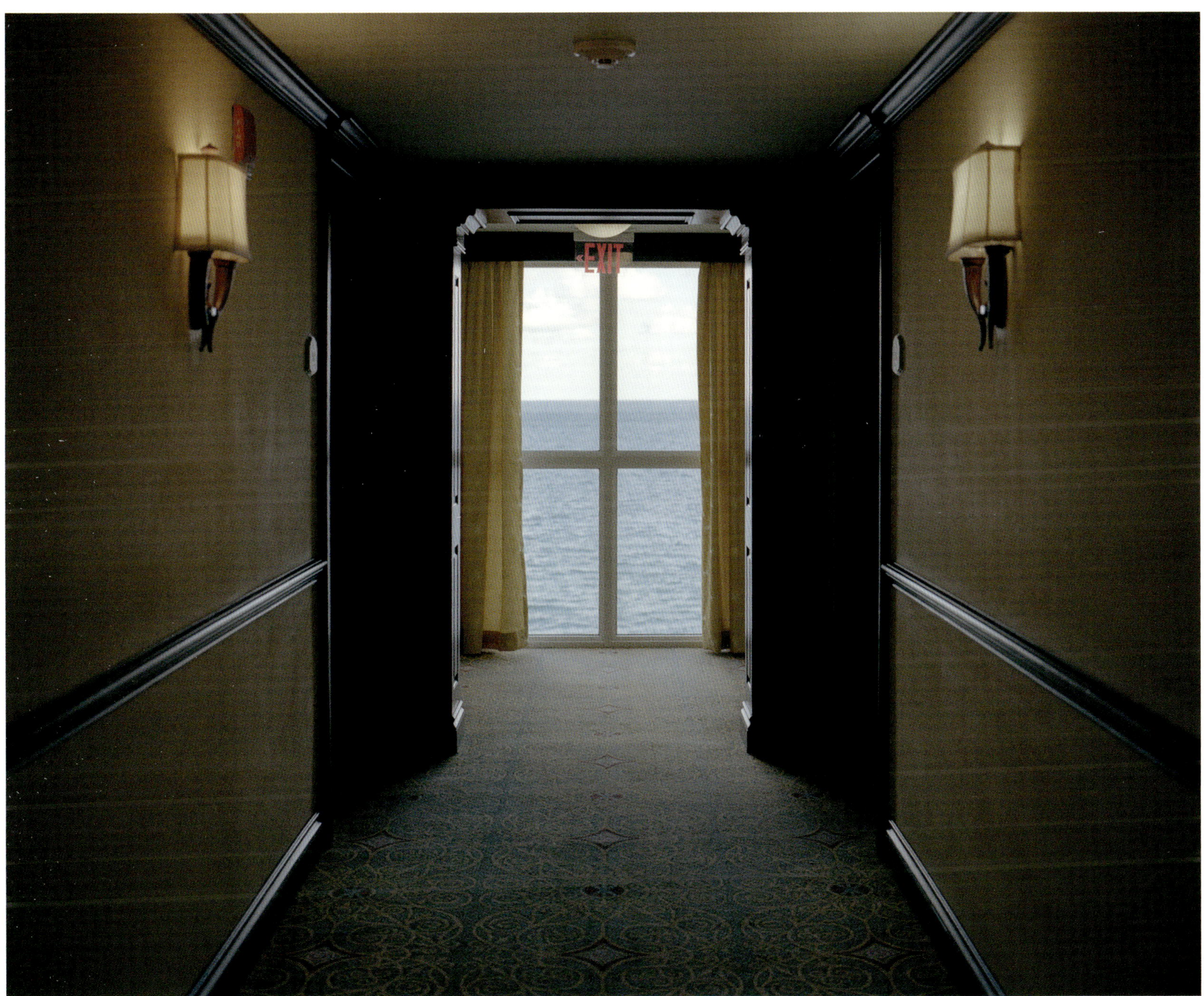

EXIT

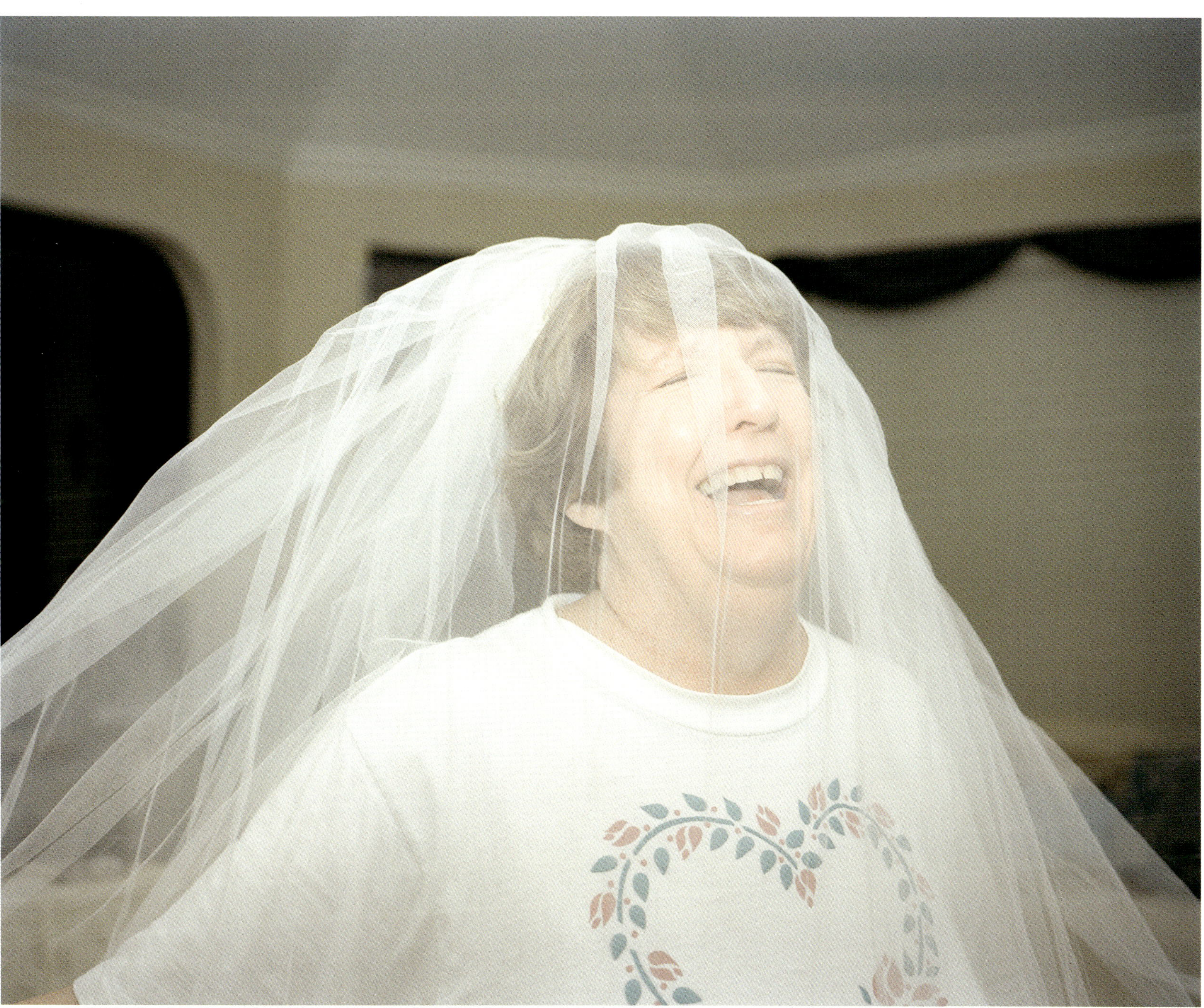

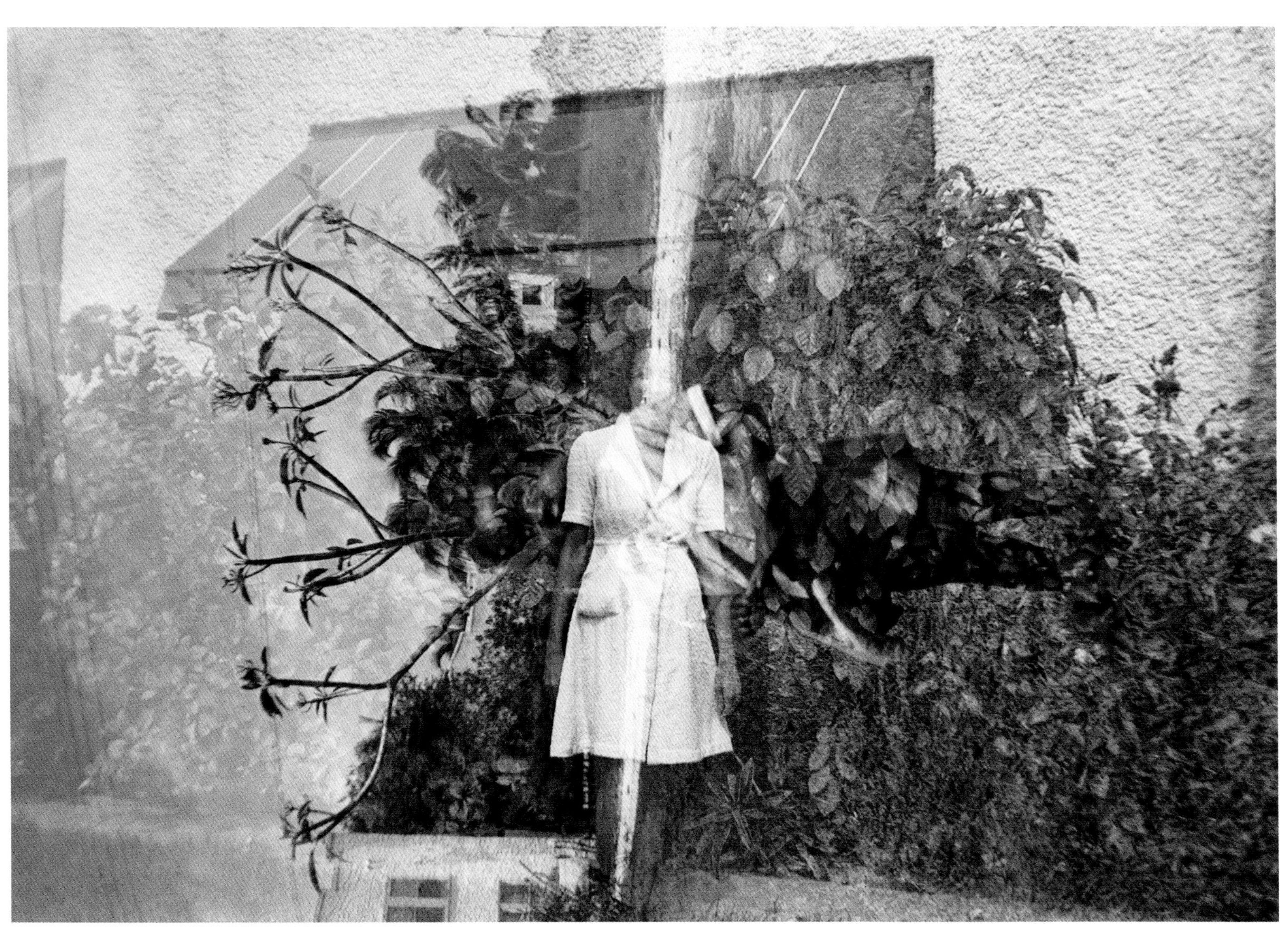

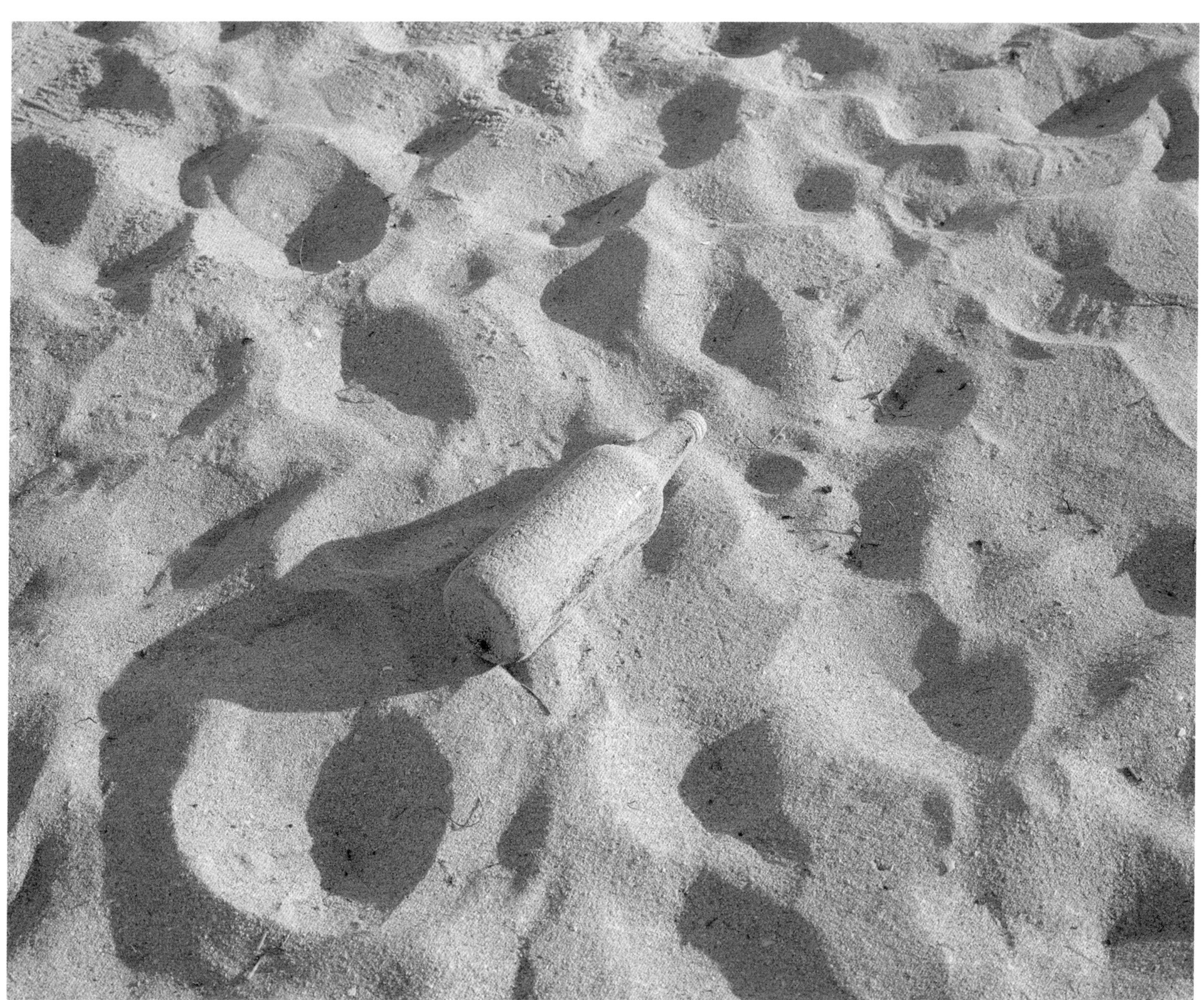

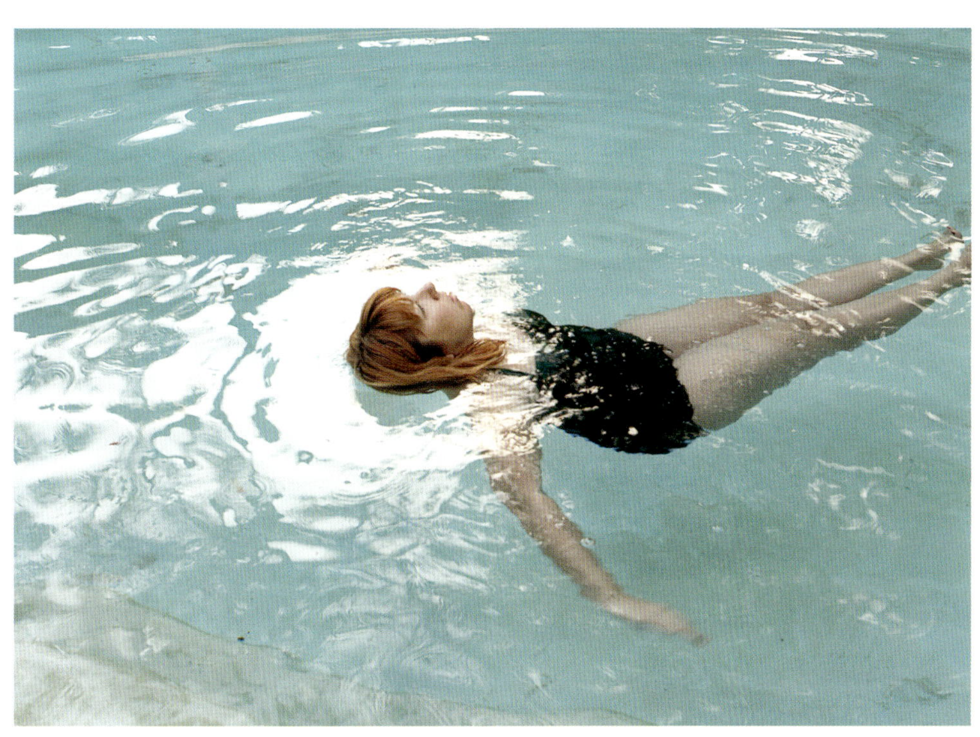

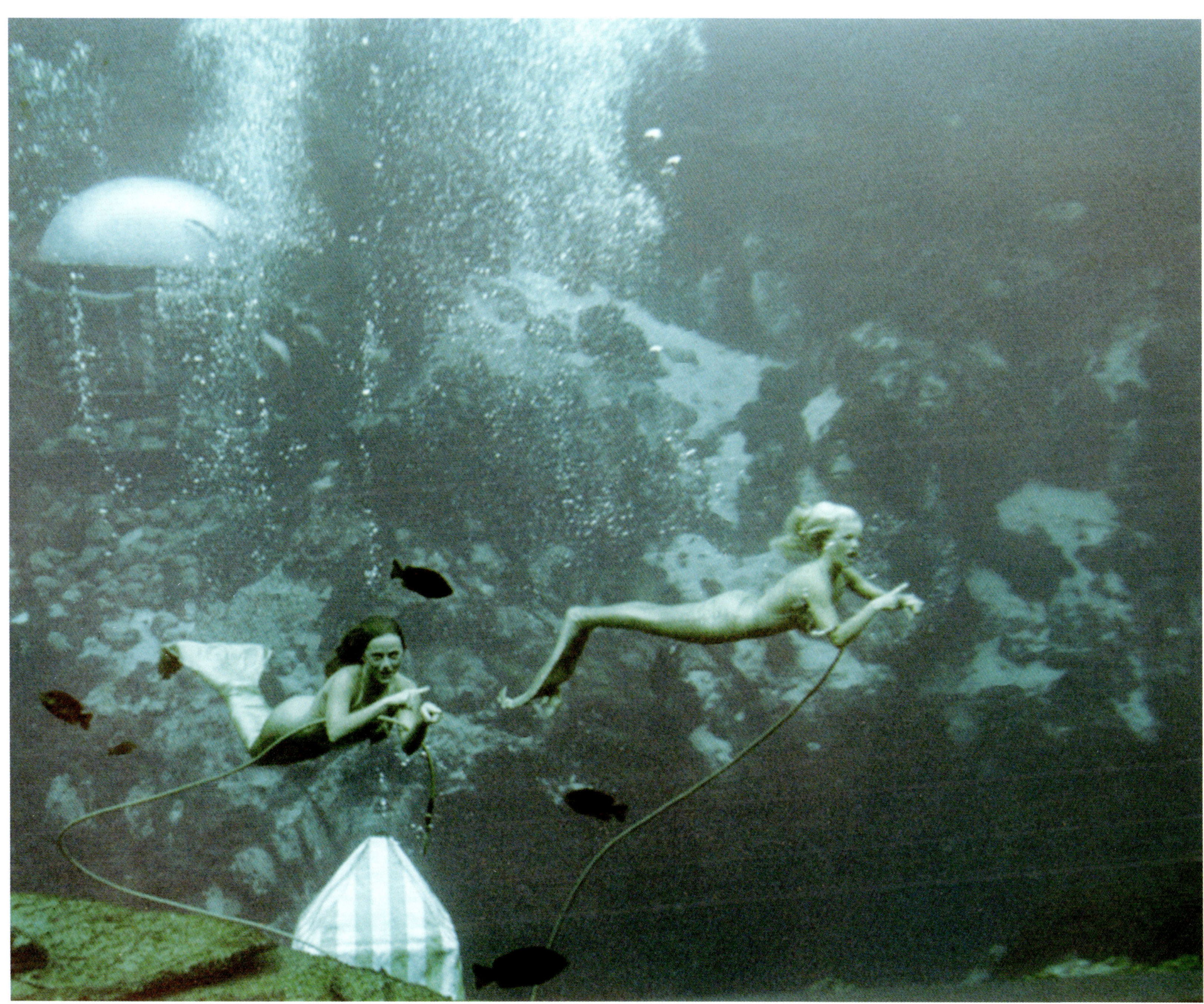

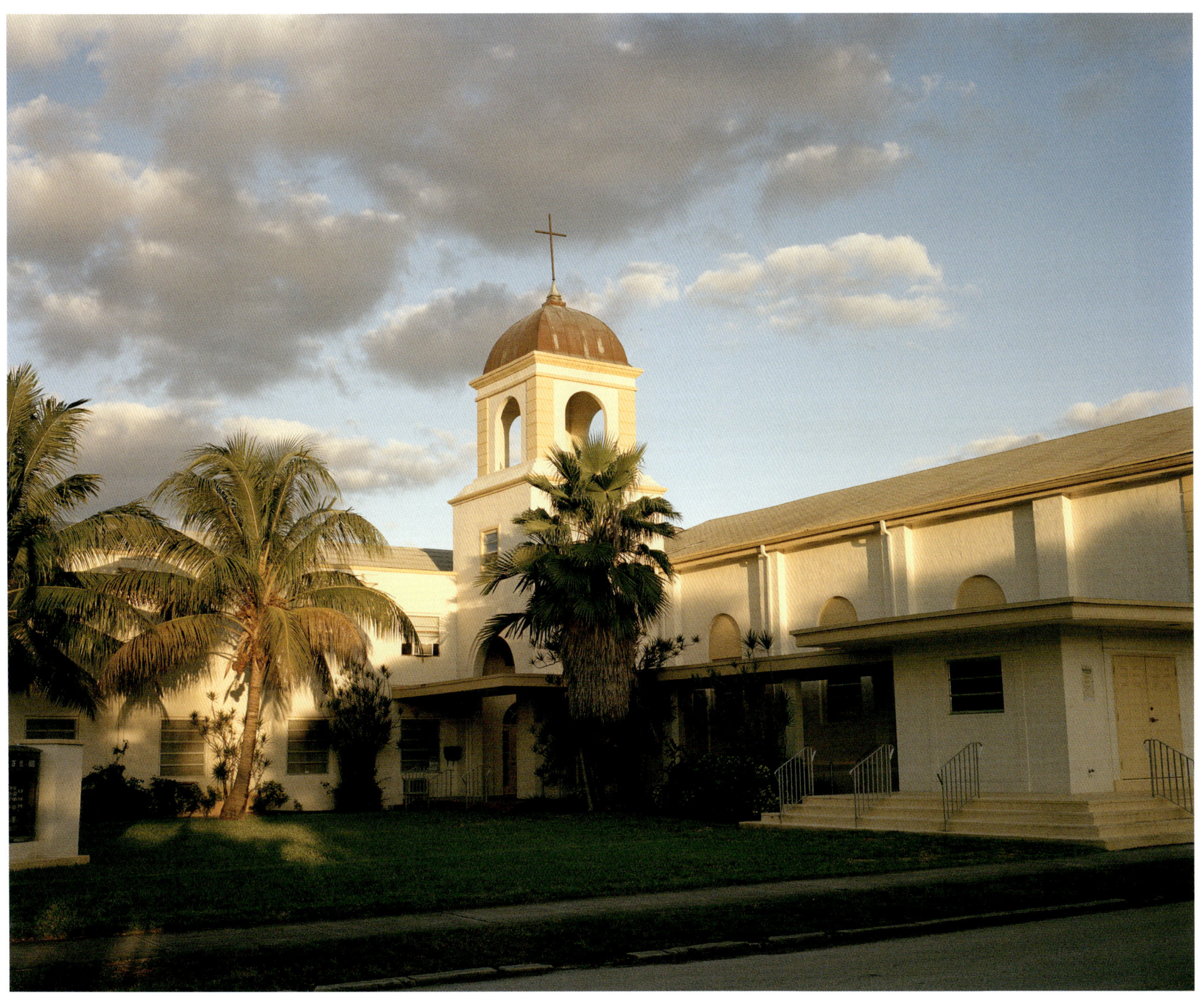

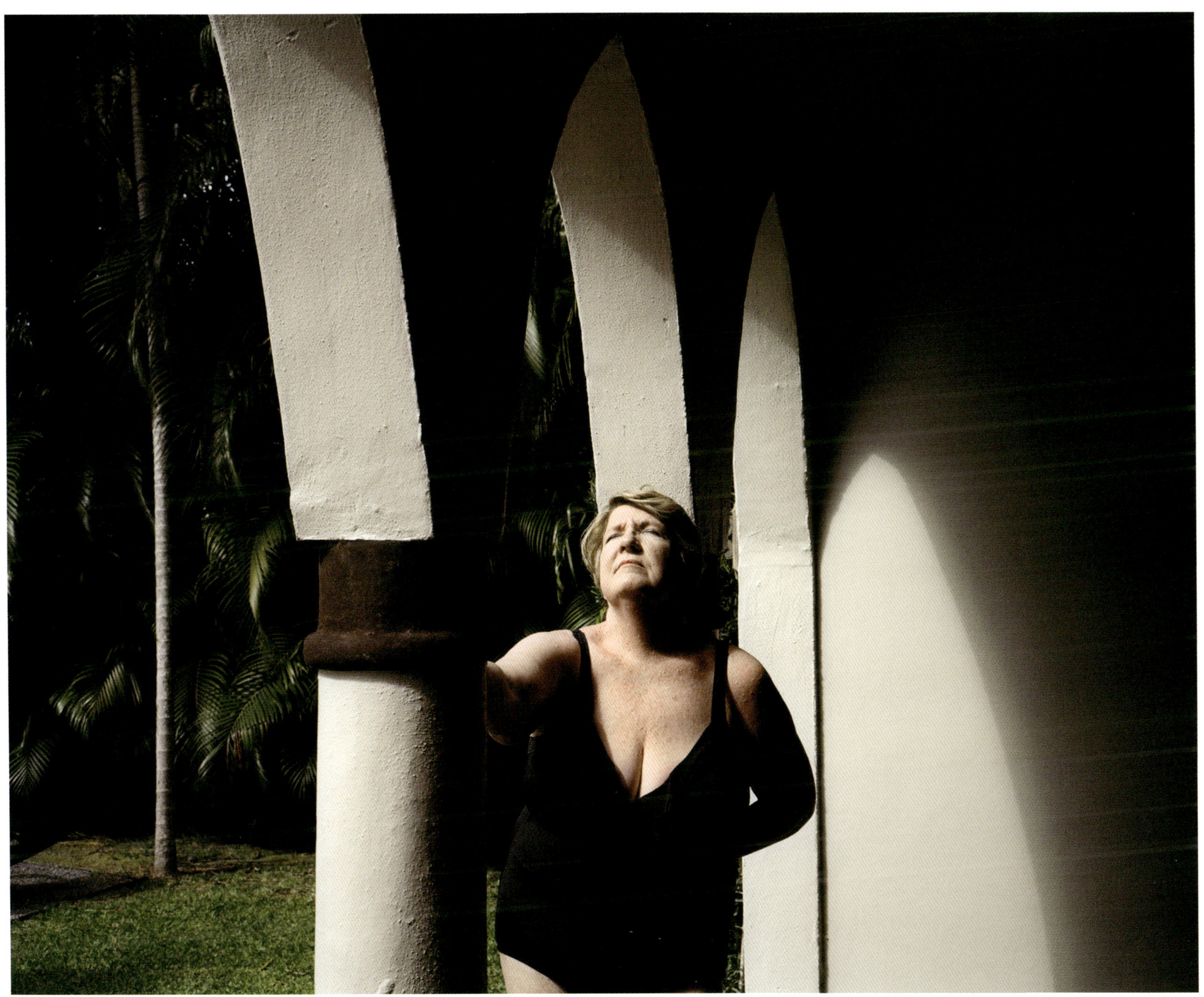

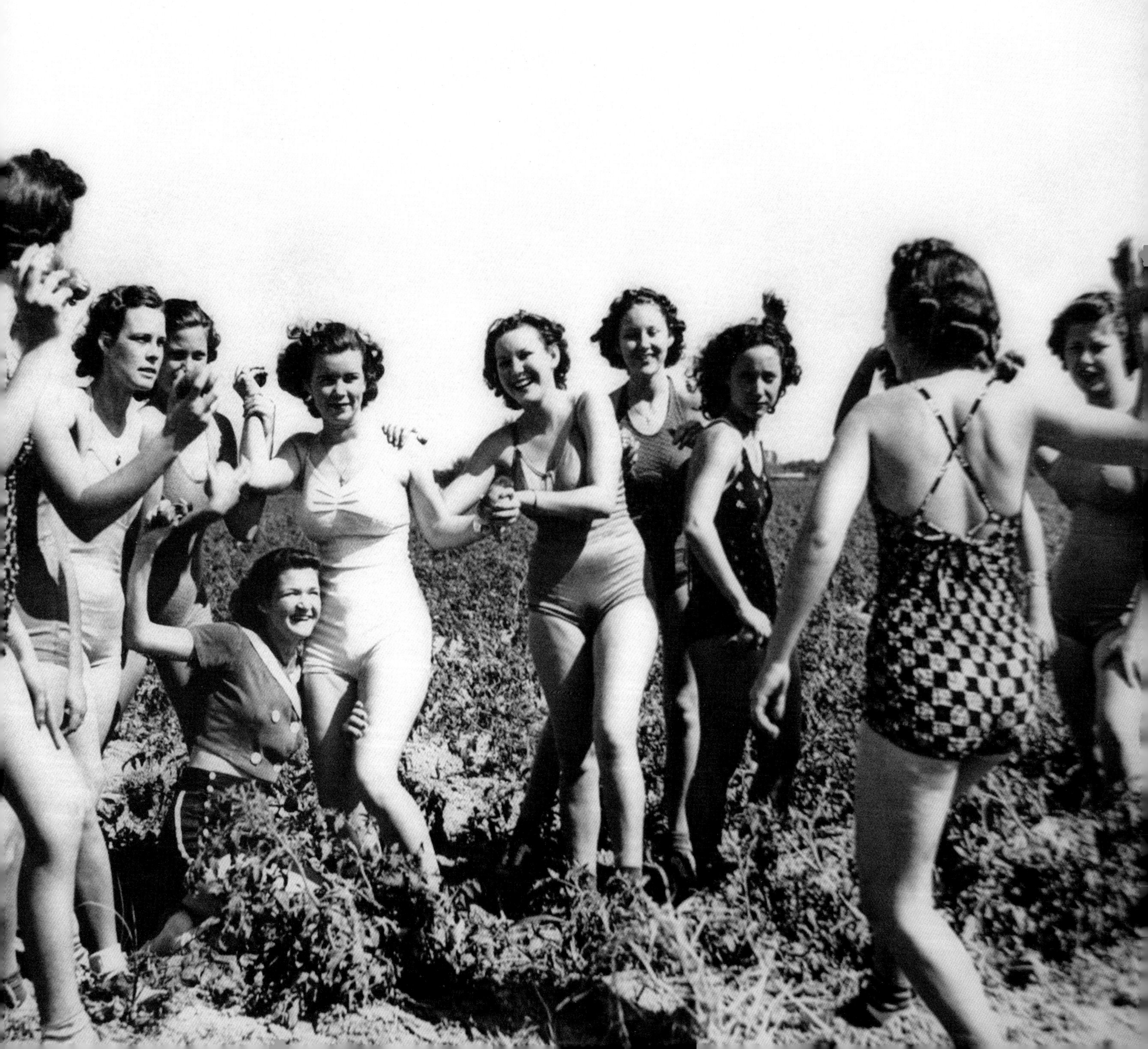

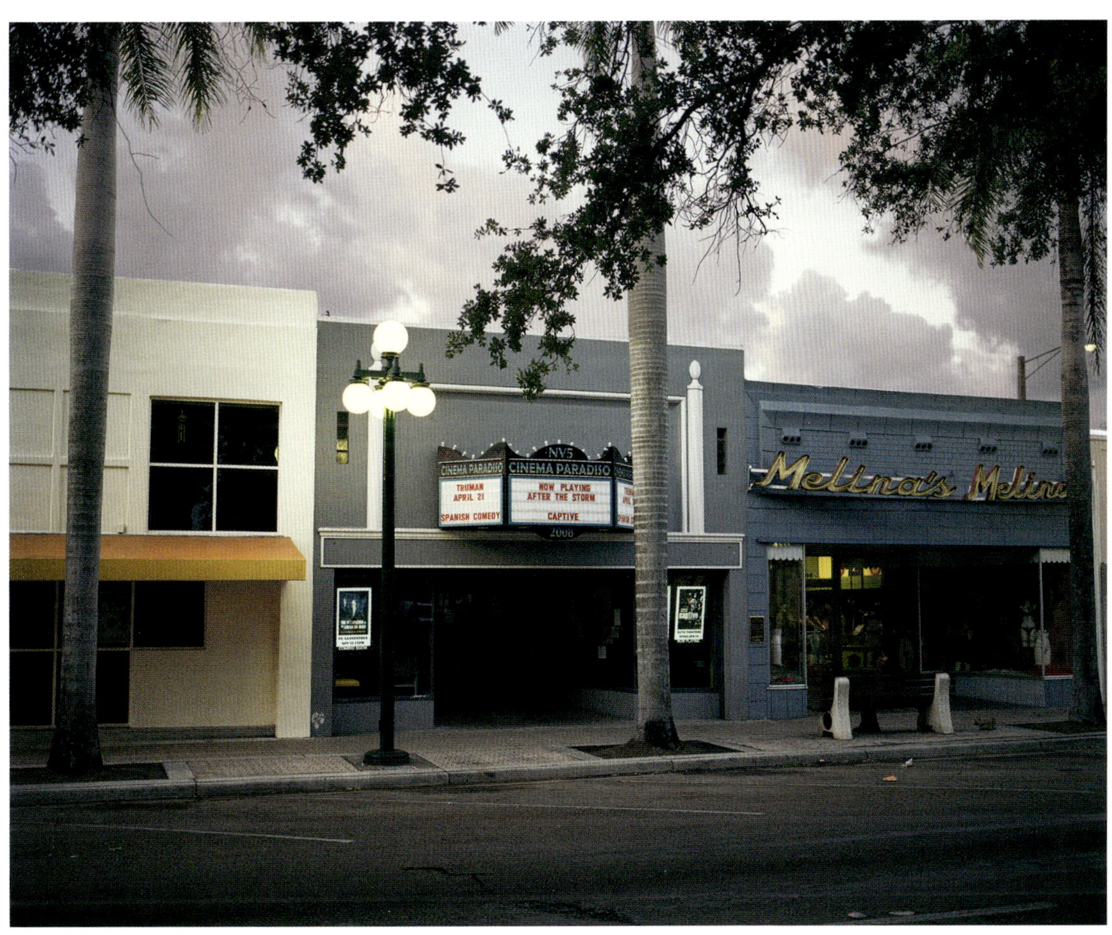
NV5
CINEMA PARADISO
CINEMA PARADISO
TRUMAN
APRIL 21
NOW PLAYING
AFTER THE STORM
SPANISH COMEDY
CAPTIVE
2008
Melina's
Melina

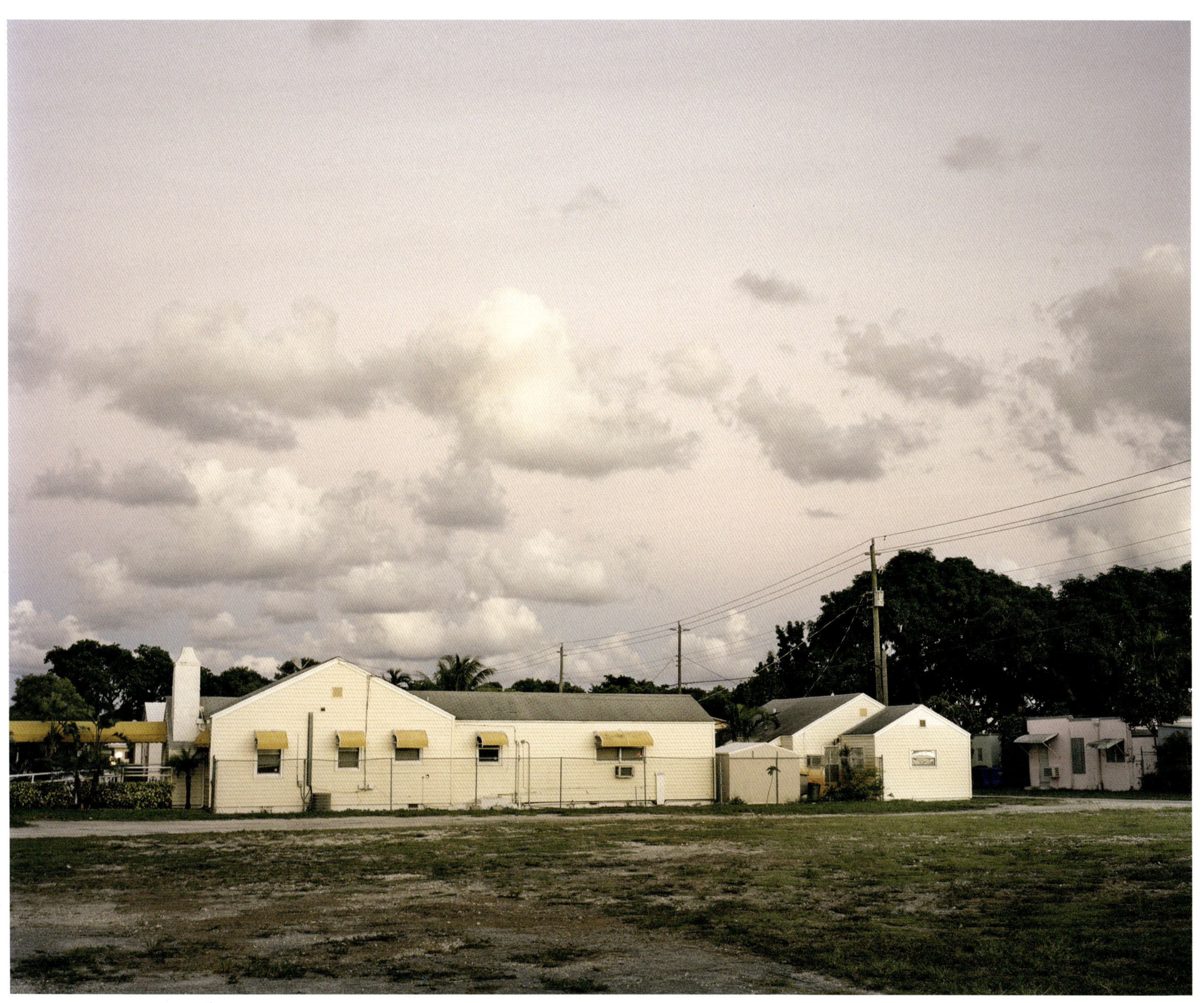

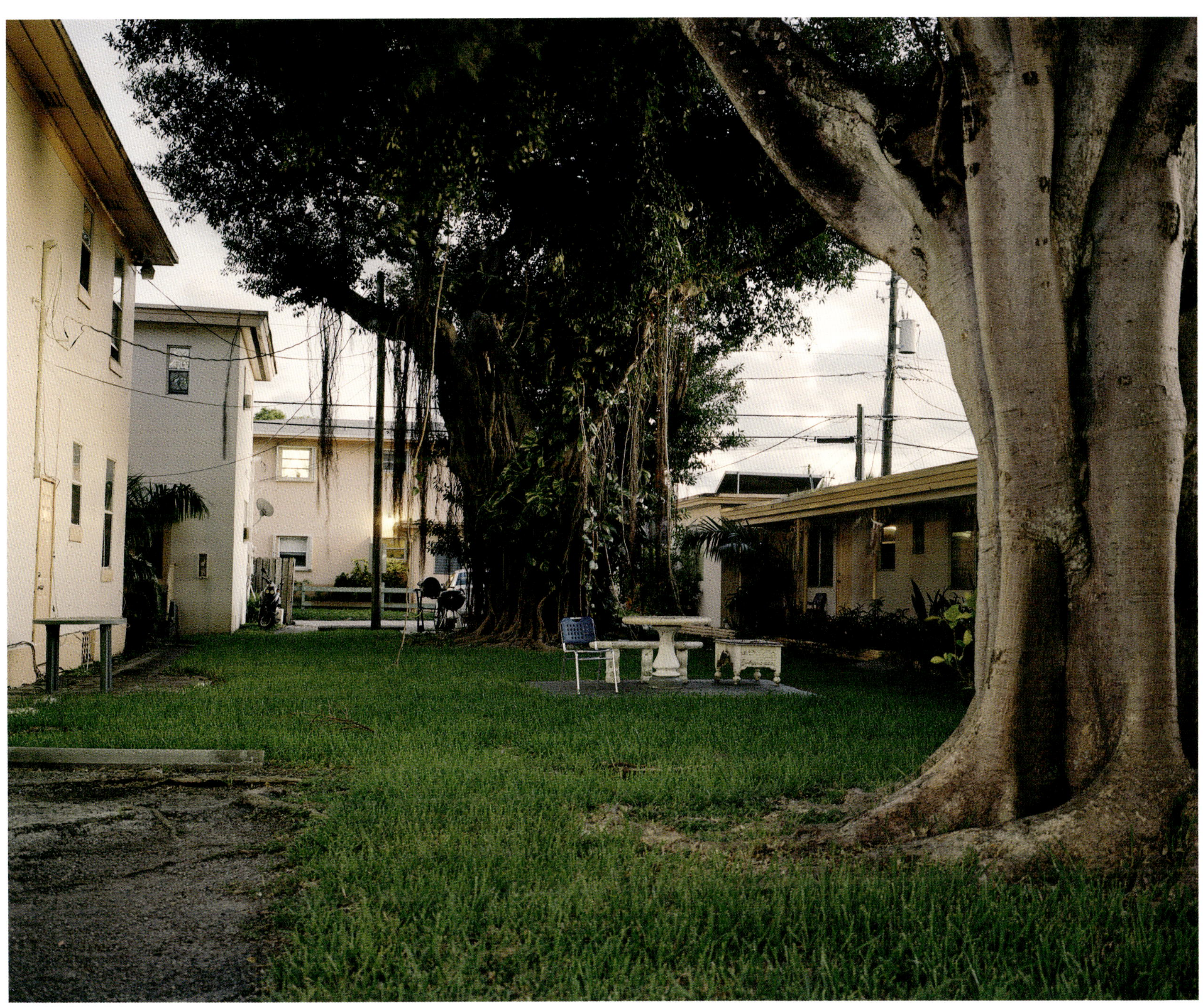

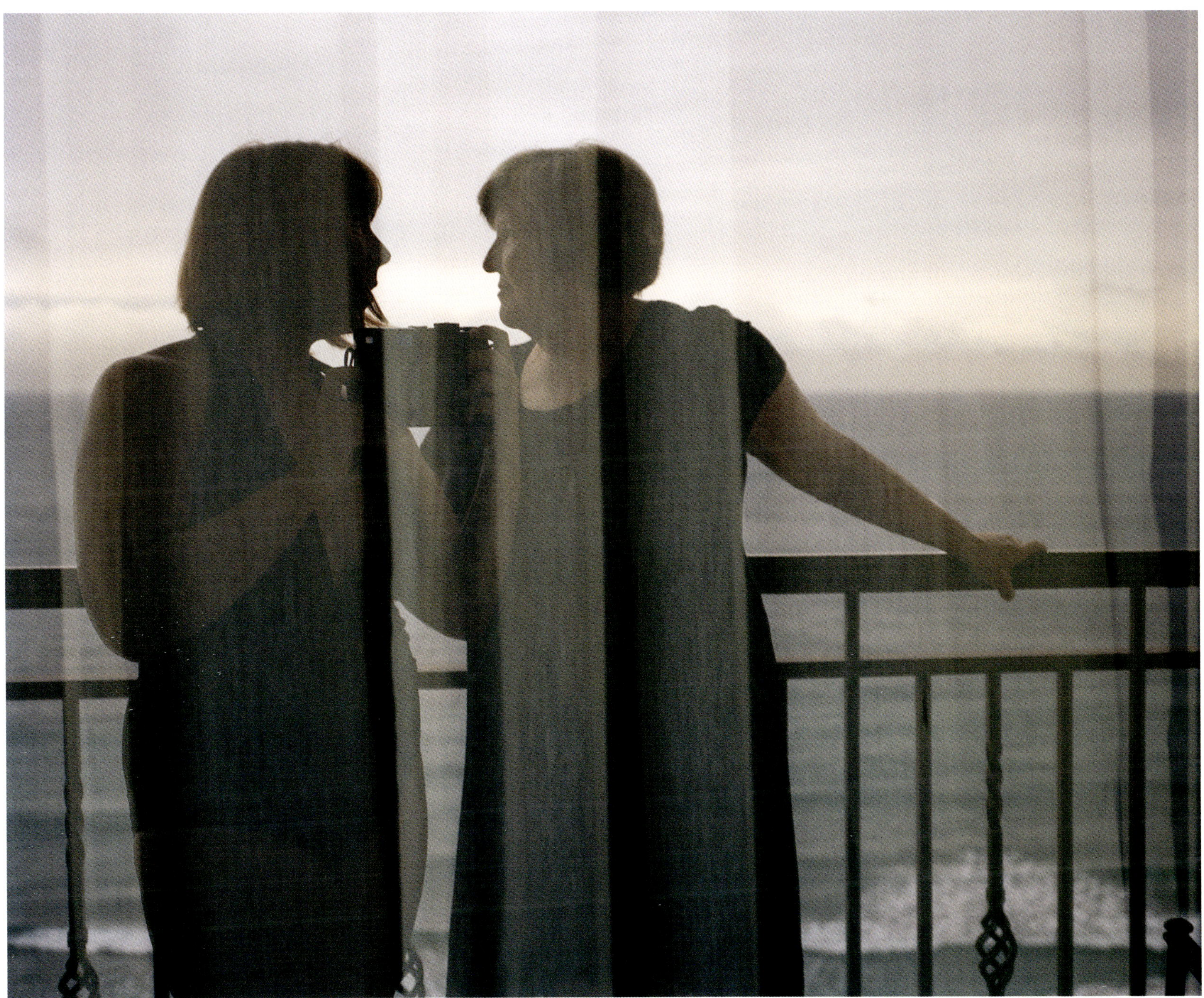

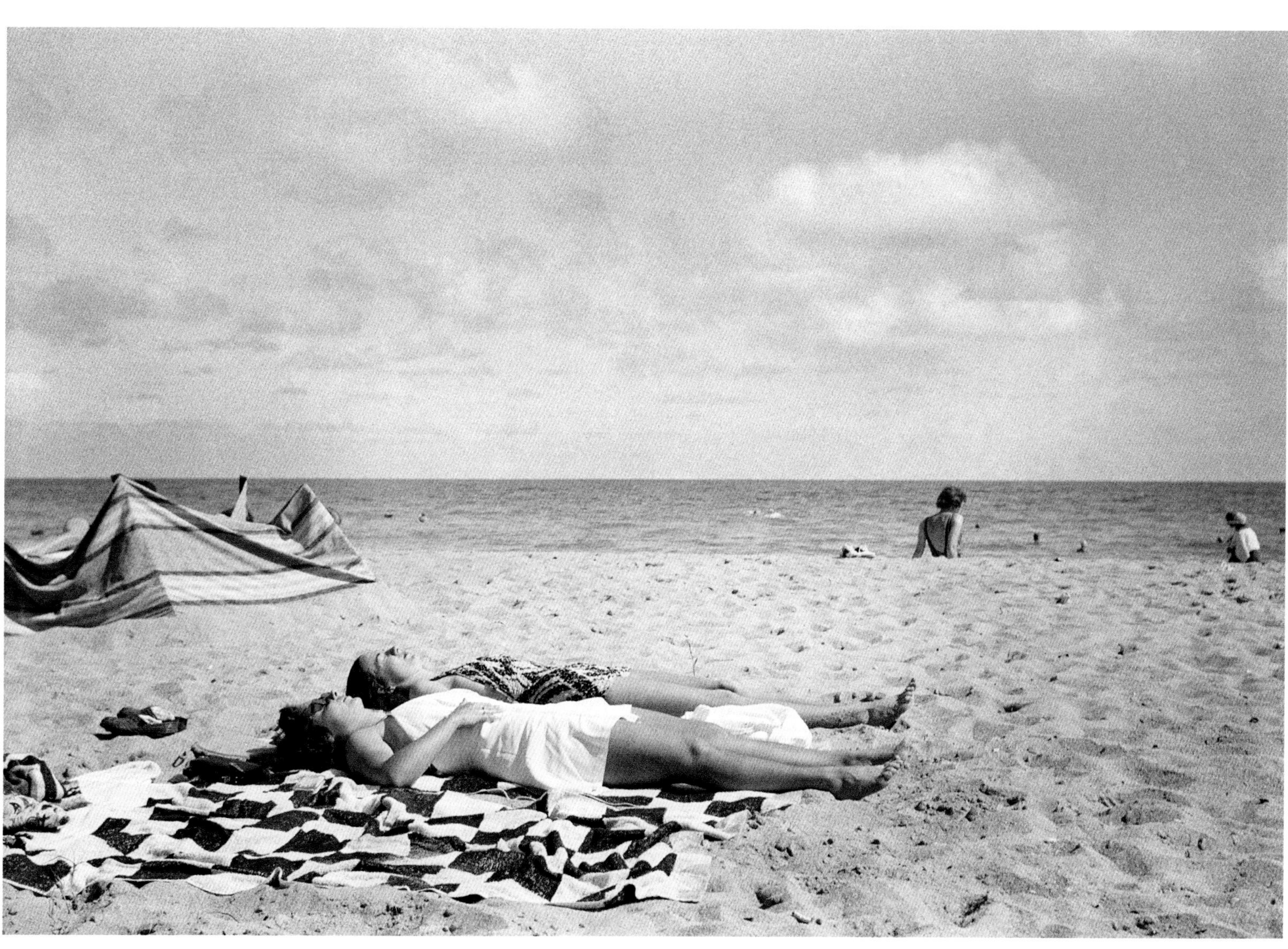

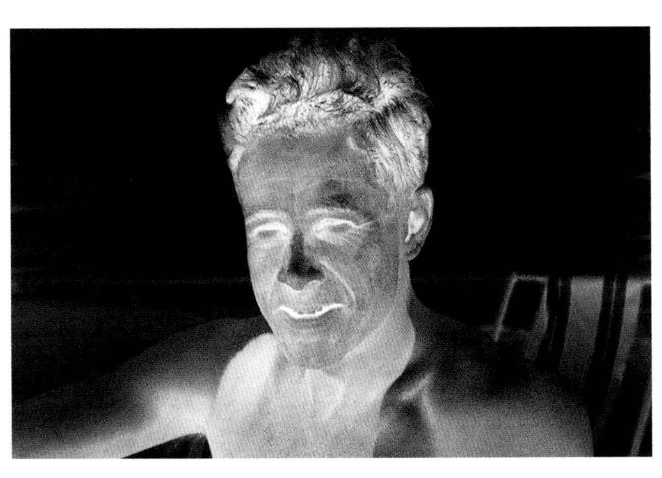 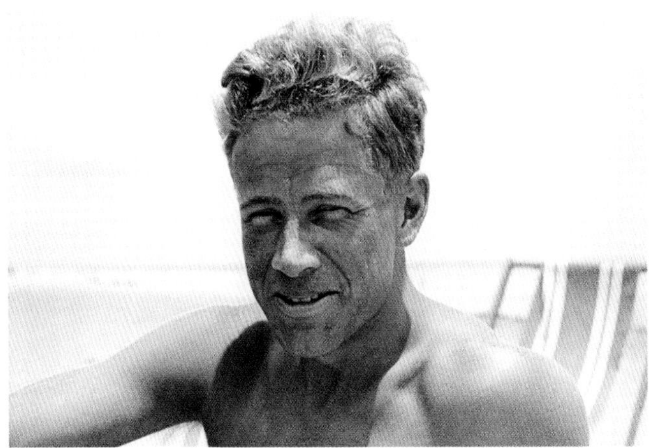

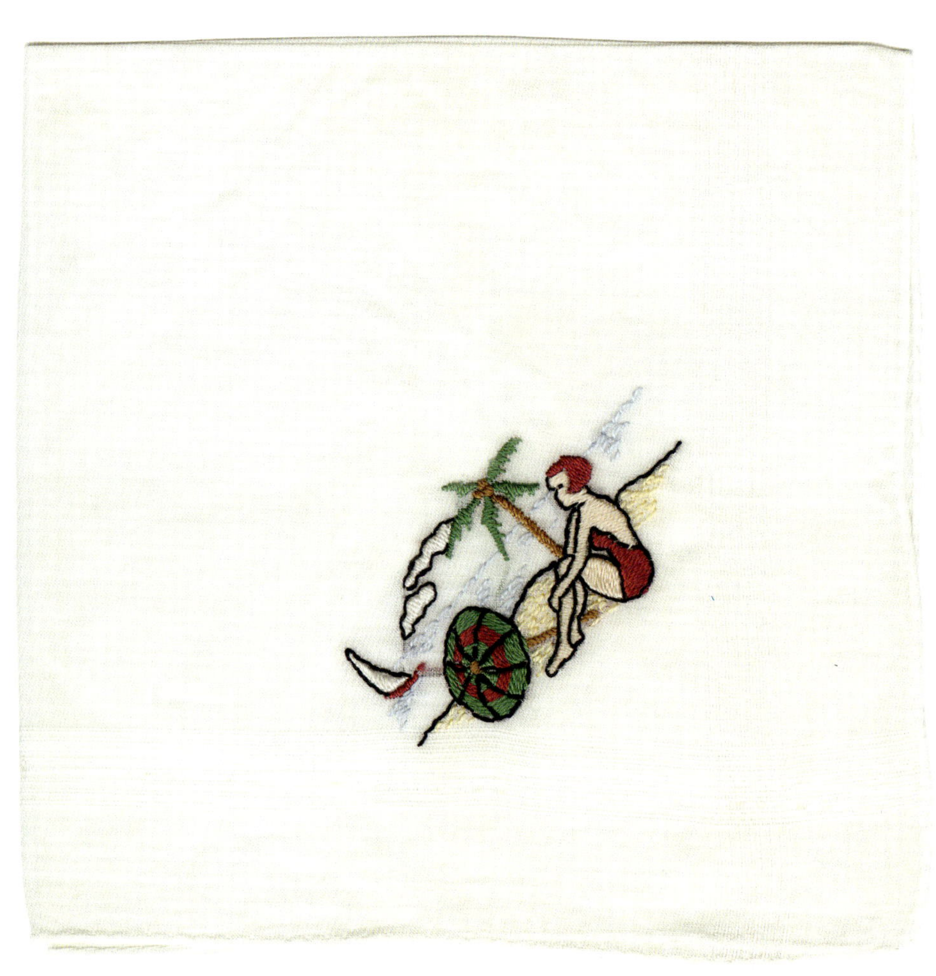

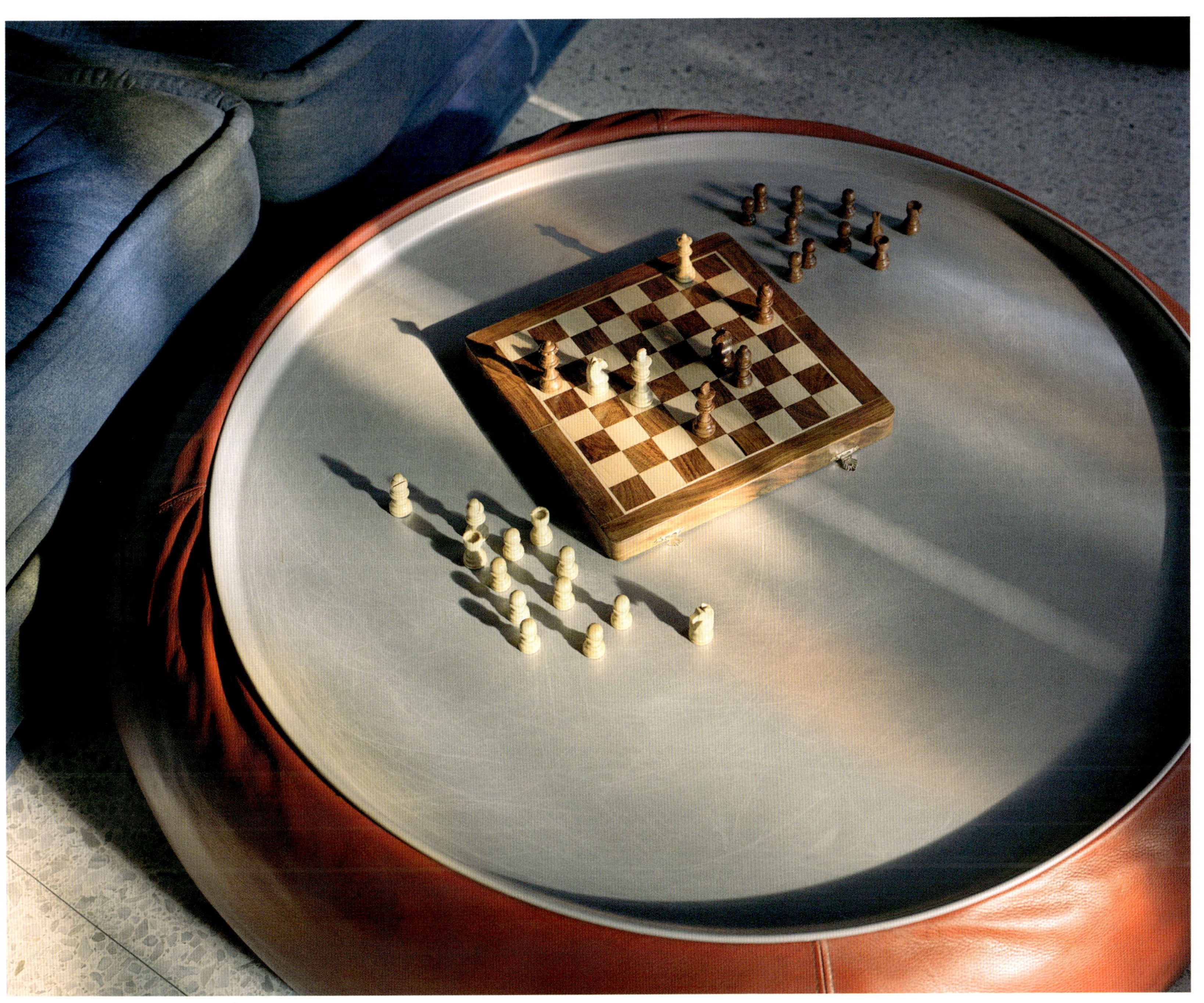

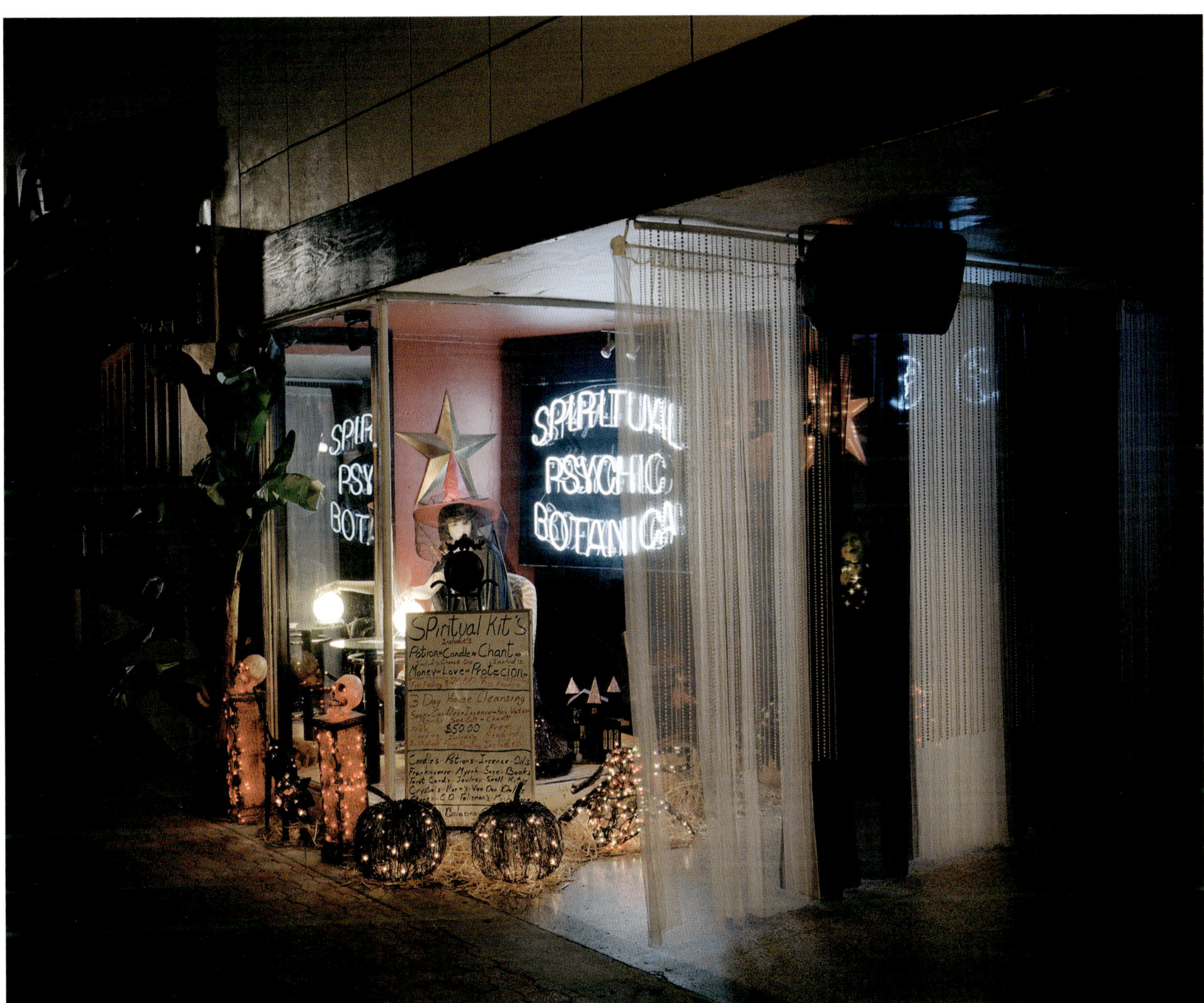

SPIRITUAL
PSYCHIC
BOTANICA
Spiritual Kit's
Include's
Potion - Candle - Chant
Money - Love - Protecion
3 Day House Cleansing
$50.00
Candle's - Potions - Incence - Oil's

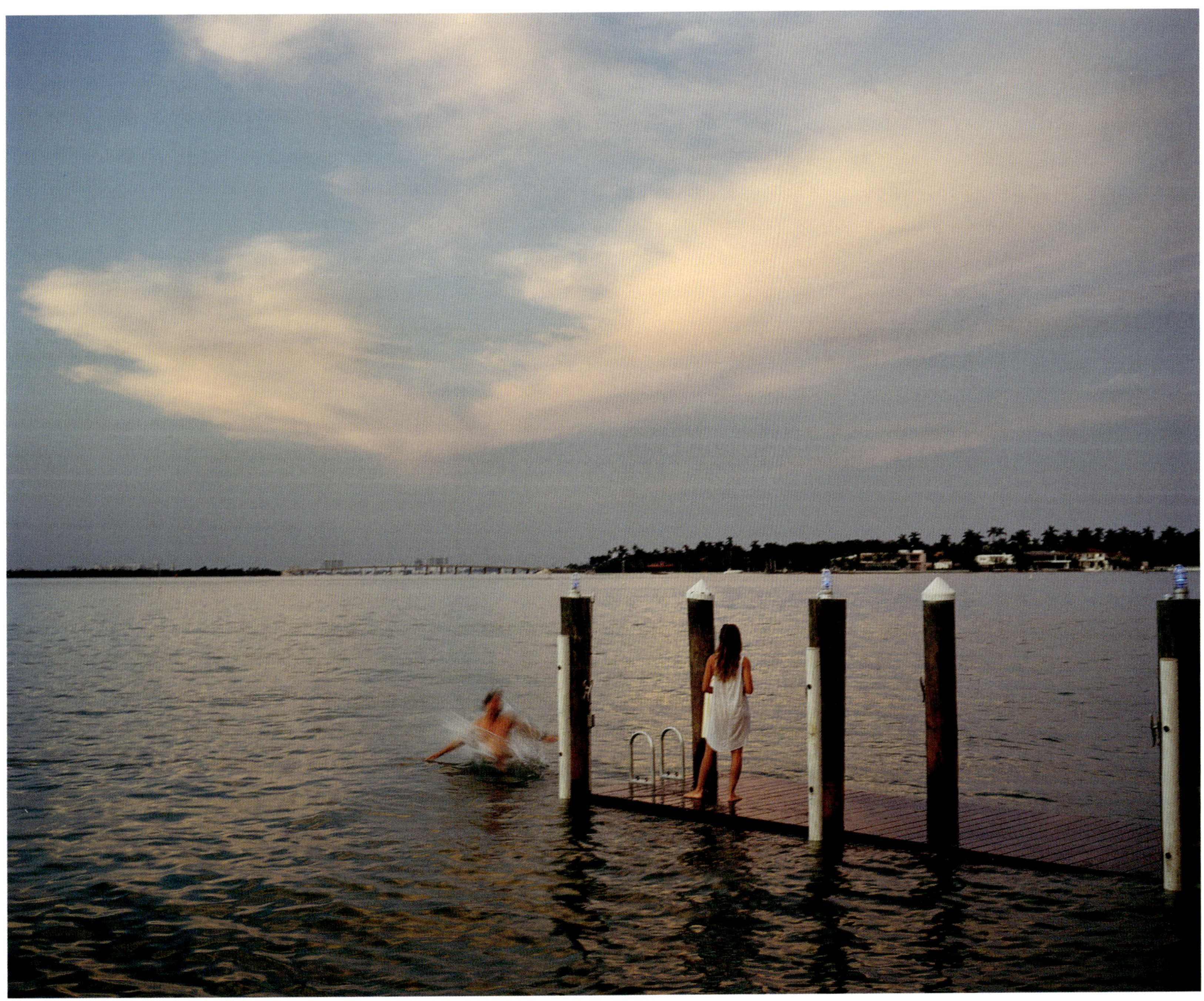

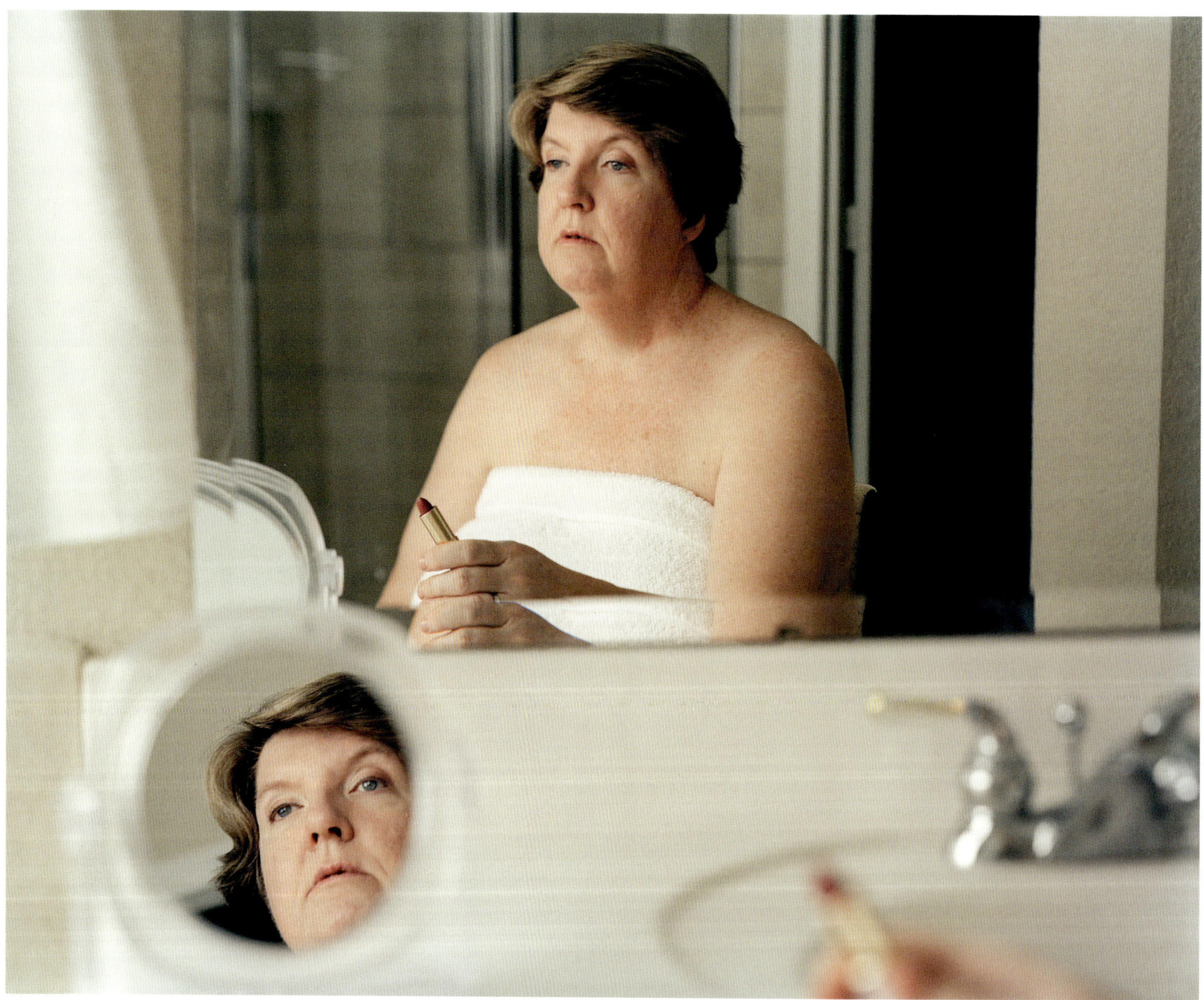

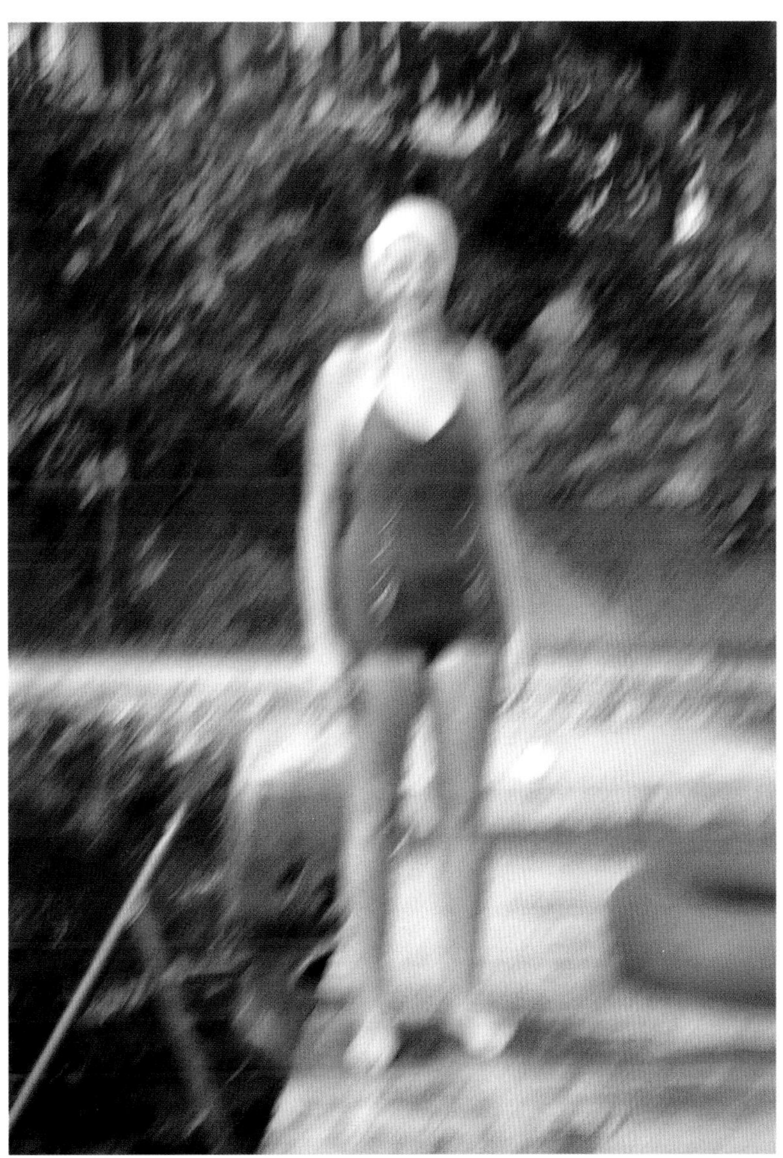

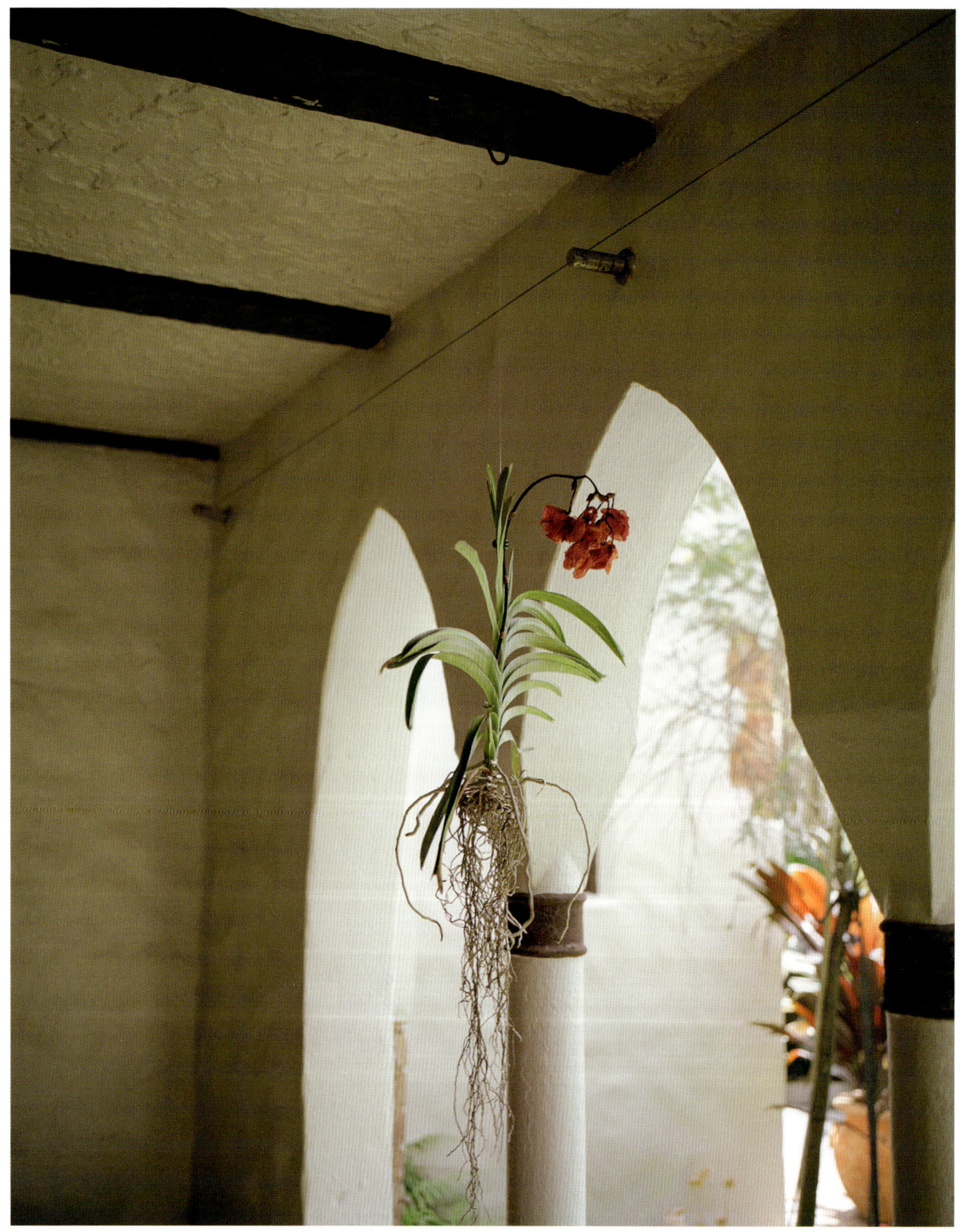

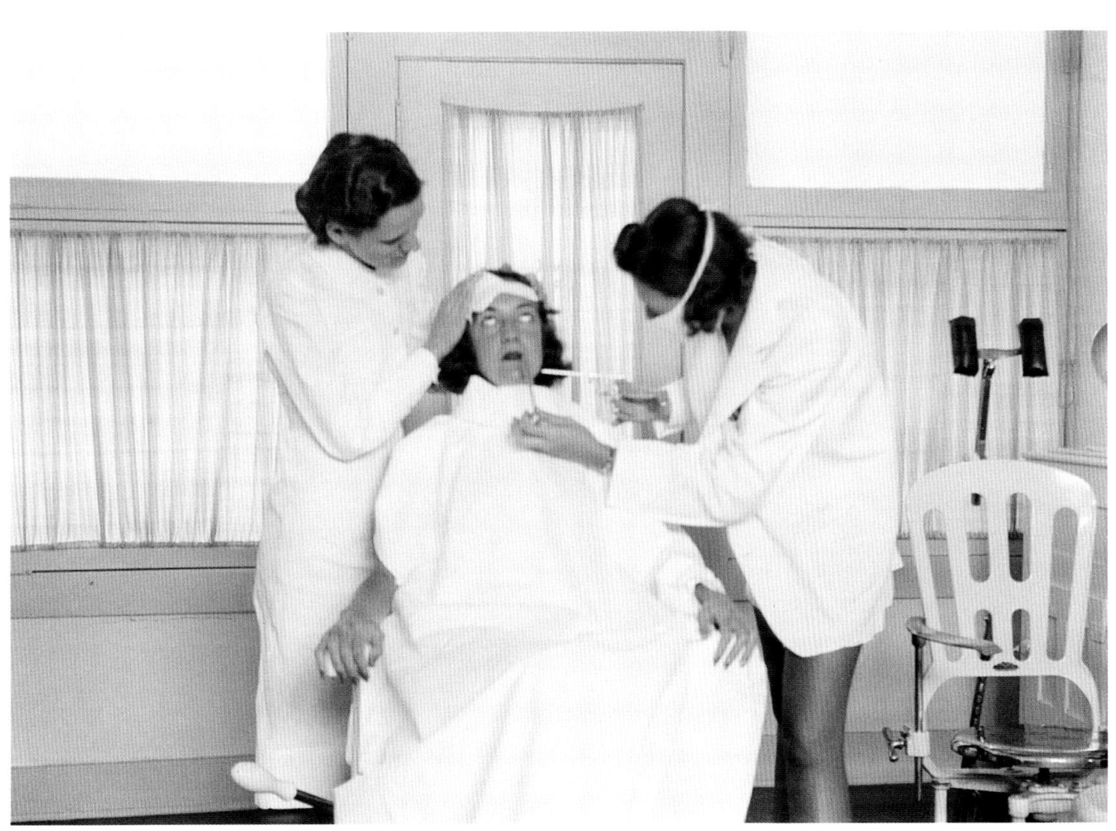

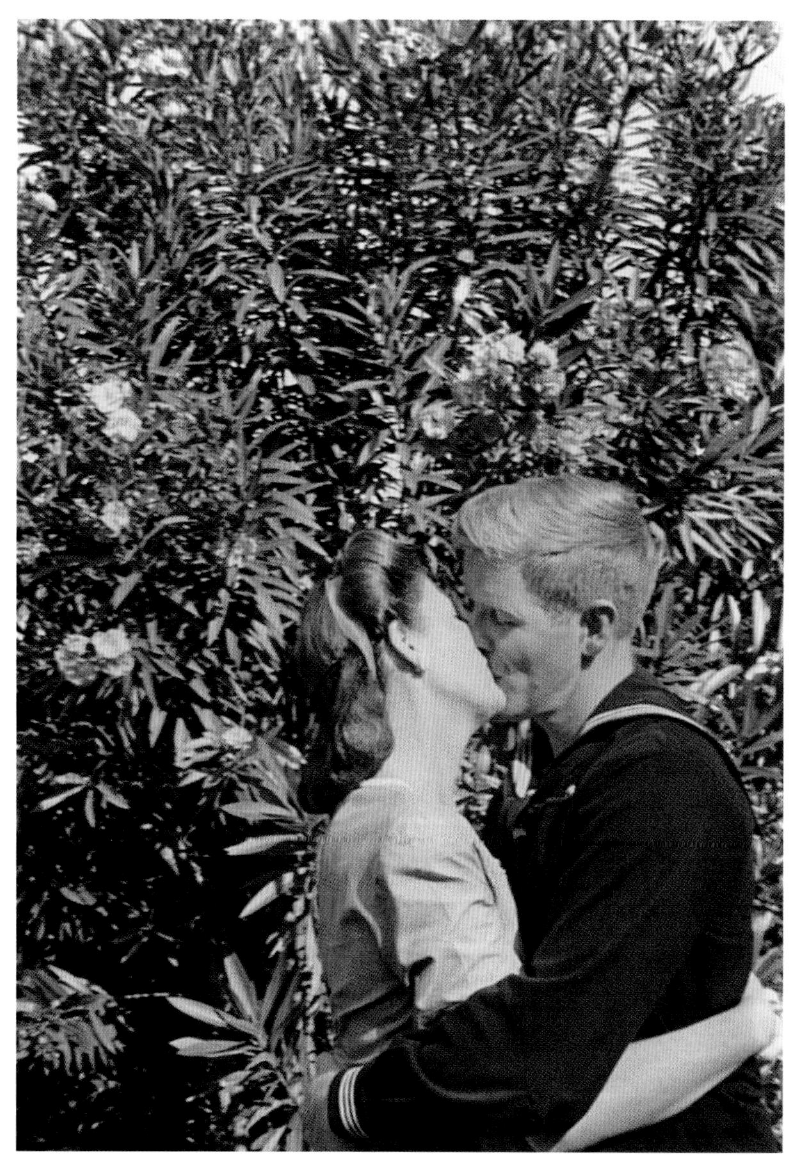

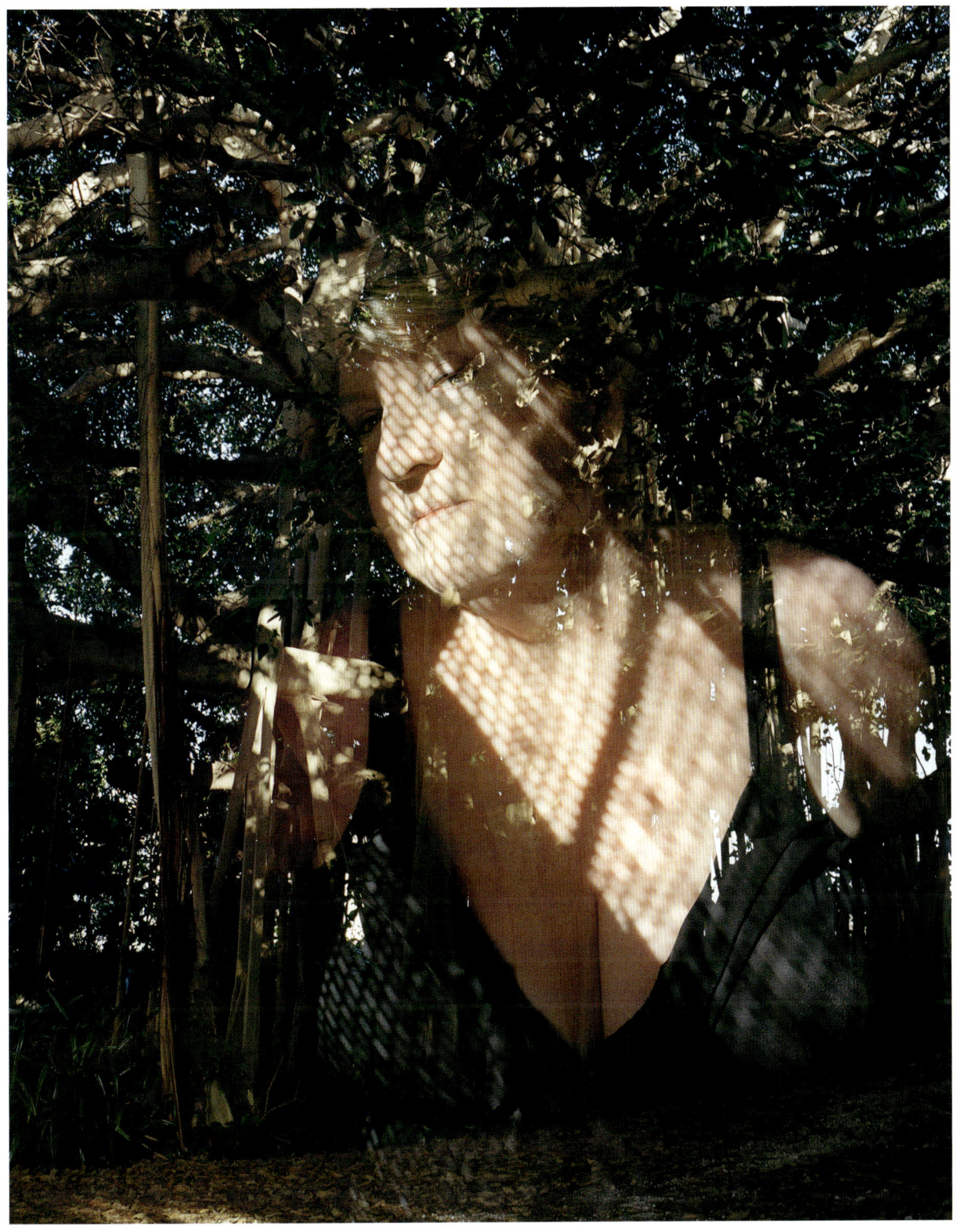

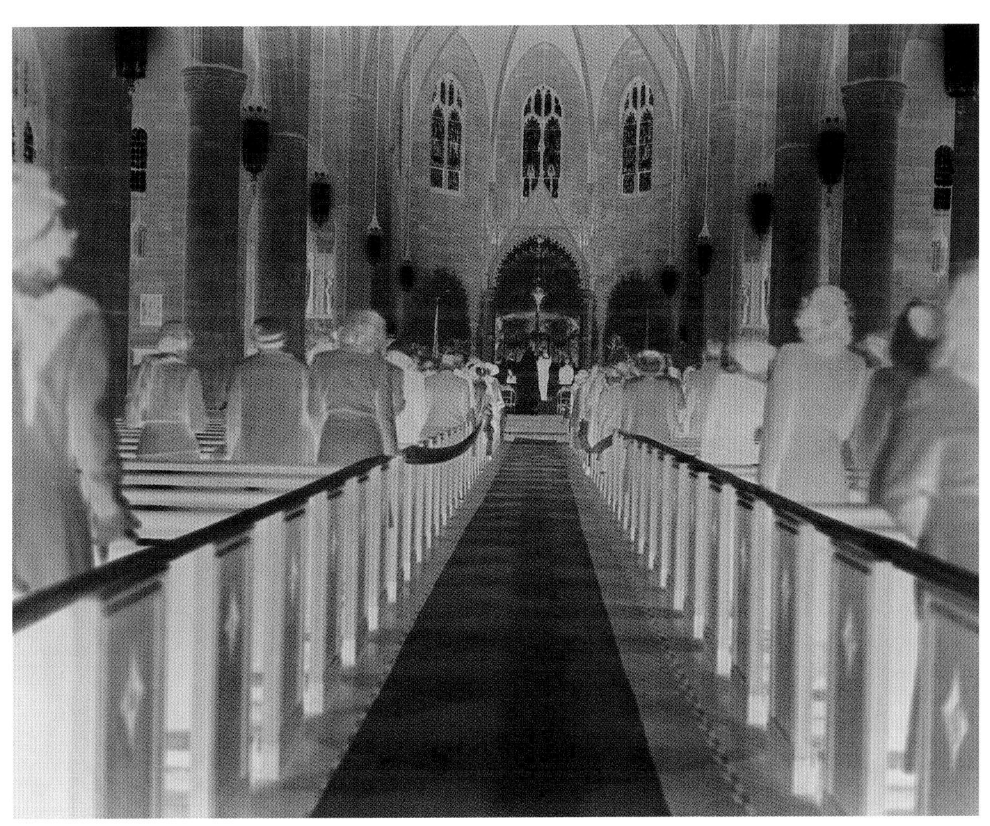

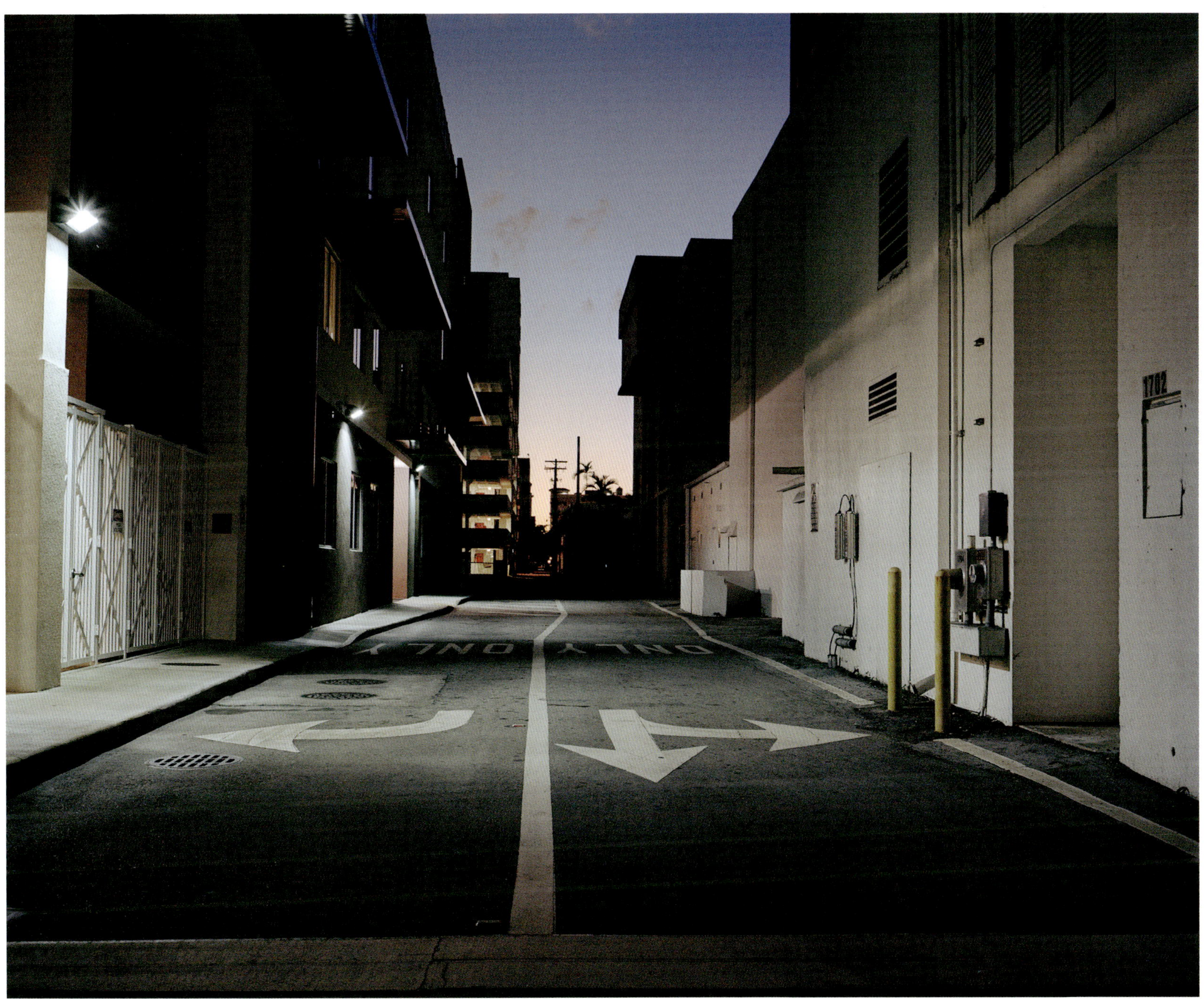
ONLY ONLY
1702

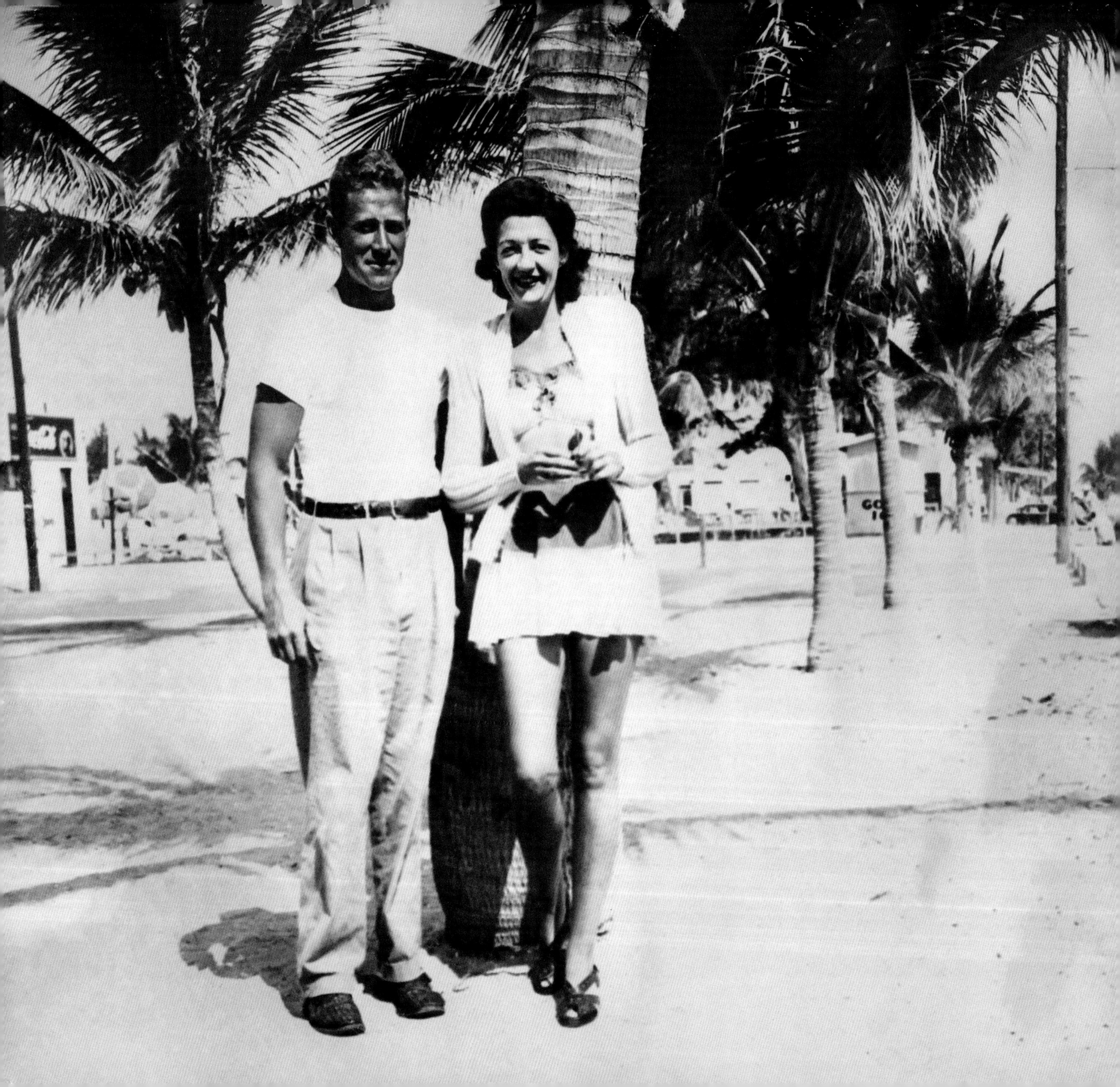

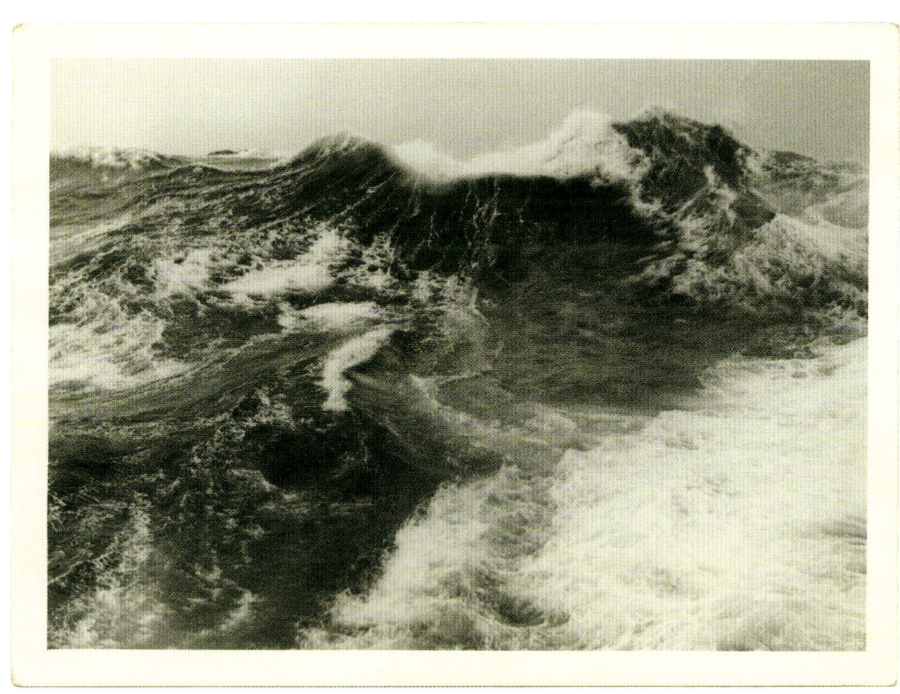

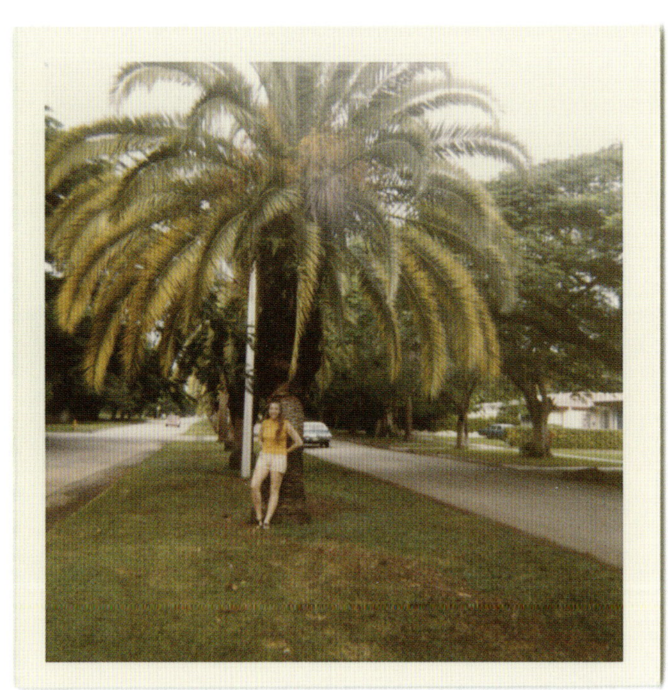

Dear Carolyn,

Your secrets are not safe with me. I've never been good at keeping secrets, except my own.

When I look at the photos you took so long ago, all I can think is, "Who could blame you?" If I had just spent the last year driving an ambulance for the Red Cross while the world was at war, I would probably want to run away to a beach, fall in love with a handsome priest, and marry a crinkly blue-eyed sailor too. Hollywood was your escape. It became mine too.

The photos of Father Jim that you took on the beach when he was so young and gorgeous make me want to whisper in your ear, "I know." And, "If it's any consolation, he'll be there through it all: from when you walk down that aisle towards him as you marry Grandpa to when you pass the pews so many years later in your coffin."

We had been returning to this beach to make our photographs for years before Mom told me she had her own fling here a decade before I was born. His name was John. She showed me her yellowed snapshots from that trip and the love-sick letter she wrote her sister about him. That was around the same time she asked me, "Do you want to know how many of us are bipolar?"

In my fantasy, you're an open book. We sip whiskey on that cobwebbed metal glider in the veranda, eating petit fours from Trost's as the cicadas hum outside. I ask you what it was like to have a mother who was bipolar and what happened the day you found her.

In reality, you held your cards to your chest. Mom has her theories about what broke inside of you. Mine are more forgiving. None of us get through it unscathed, and magnets with the same polarity always repel each other.

Your photos told me what I needed to know. I heard you and replied. We talked about fate and desire, solitude and secrets, mothers and daughters, and the ocean tides that bind us.

Fair winds,
Sara

ACKNOWLEDGMENTS

This book is dedicated to my mother Kathleen Quinn Macel. Thank you for your trust, patience, and collaboration making these images and telling our story. 1.4.3. I owe tremendous gratitude to my beloved uncle Thomas Quinn for being the catalyst behind this work. Until we meet again on the other shore, T.Q. Special thanks to Patricia Quinn-Munson for our invaluable talks about our family history. Thank you to my father, Dennis Macel, my sisters Connie Leininger & Andrea Osorio and their families, and all my extended family for their love and support always.

A heartfelt thank you to the photographic community who has promoted this work through exhibitions, awards, and publications. Thank you Sarah Simms, Marvin Heiferman, Ashlyn Davis Burns, Maureen Drennan, Adair Freeman Rutledge, Kris Graves, Light Work (John Mannion, Shane Lavalette, Mary Lee Hodgens, Rachel Fein-Smolinski, Julie Herman, Rebecca Marris, Gabe Conte), Eileen MacAvery-Kane, Juliana Forero, Aline Smithson, Jennifer Yoffy, Odette England, Jennifer Garza-Cuen, Andrew Fedynak, Cynthia Bittenfield, Nat Ward, Siobhán Bohnacker, Jenny Riffle, Liz Arenberg, Dina Mitrani, Roy Flukinger, Mary Virginia Swanson, David Bram, Kate Mackey, Tara Kennedy, Morgan Hallett, Anne Cardenas, Nichole Aiello, Mikey Post, Steve McCarthy, Wassaic Project, and Marble Hill Camera Club.

I am so grateful to Cooper Winterson and Gerard Franciosa of My Own Color Lab, whose retouching skills and good company are unmatched. The Hollywood Historical Society, Broward County Clerk's Office, The Diocesan Archives, and the Art and Culture Center Hollywood were vital resources while researching this project.

Thank you to Alexa Becker and Klaus Kehrer for believing in this project and bringing me into the fold. Many thanks to Daniel Sommer, Sylvia Ballhause, Erik Clewe, and the entire Kehrer Verlag team for their exquisite work. My deepest thanks to Nick Antonich for his staggering talent and for being my sounding board throughout the process of designing this book.

As always, thank you to my husband Michael Catanese for everything.

© 2022 Kehrer Verlag Heidelberg and Sara Macel

Project Management:
Kehrer Verlag (Sylvia Ballhause)

Texts:
Sara Macel

Copy Editing:
Michael Catanese

Proofreading:
Michael Catanese, Sarah Simms

Design:
Kehrer Design (Nick Antonich), Sara Macel

Image Processing:
Kehrer Design (Erik Clewe)

Production Management:
Kehrer Design (Tom Streicher)

Archival Images (pp. 22, 68):
Hollywood Historical Society

Bibliographic information published by the
Deutsche Nationalbibliothek
The Deutsche Nationalbibliothek lists this
publication in the Deutsche Nationalbibliografie;
detailed bibliographic data is available on the
internet at http://dnb.dnb.de.

Printed and bound in Germany
ISBN 978-3-96900-052-6

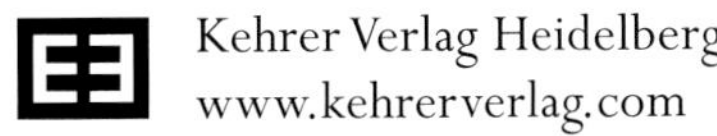

Kehrer Verlag Heidelberg
www.kehrerverlag.com

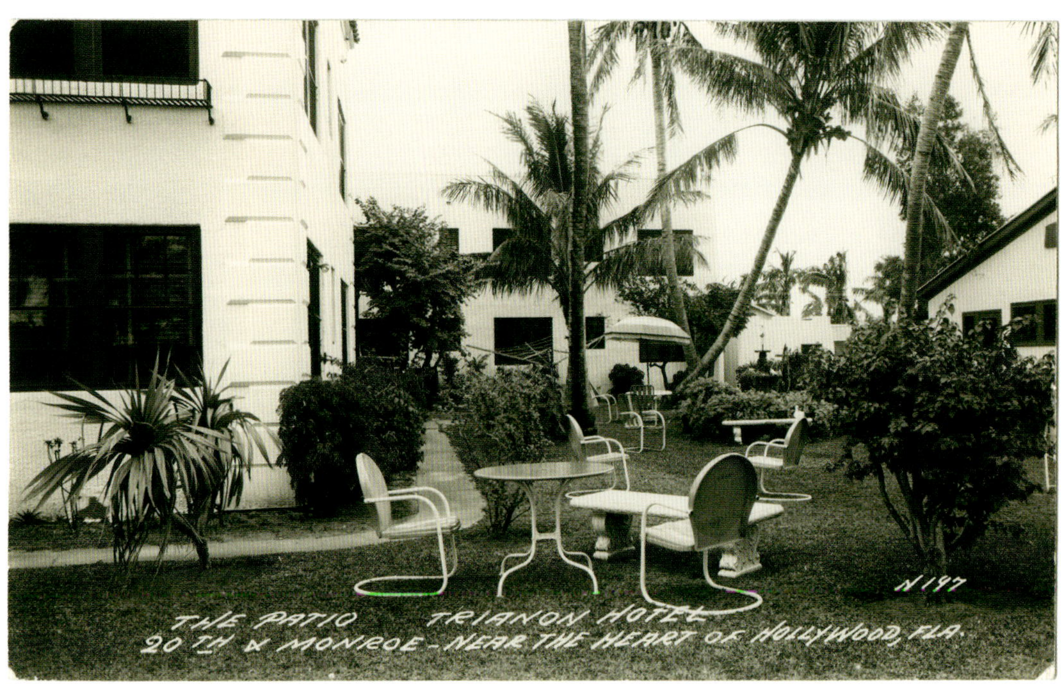

THE PATIO   TRIANON HOTEL
20 TH & MONROE - NEAR THE HEART OF HOLLYWOOD, FLA.
N 197